William H. Stewart

Catalogue of the modern masterpieces gathered by the late connoisseur William H. Stewart

William H. Stewart

Catalogue of the modern masterpieces gathered by the late connoisseur William H. Stewart

ISBN/EAN: 9783741194733

Manufactured in Europe, USA, Canada, Australia, Japa

Cover: Foto ©Andreas Hilbeck / pixelio.de

Manufactured and distributed by brebook publishing software (www.brebook.com)

WIlliam H. Stewart

Catalogue of the modern masterpieces gathered by the late connoisseur William H. Stewart

COLLECTION
OF THE LATE
W. H. STEWART

CATALOGUE

OF THE

MODERN MASTERPIECES

GATHERED BY THE LATE CONNOISSEUR

WILLIAM H. STEWART,

TO BE DISPOSED OF AT ABSOLUTE PUBLIC SALE, BY ORDER OF
HIS EXECUTORS

On Thursday and Friday Evenings, February 3D and 4th

BEGINNING AT 8.15 O'CLOCK EACH EVENING

AT CHICKERING HALL

FIFTH AVENUE AND EIGHTEENTH STREET

THE COLLECTION WILL BE ON EXHIBITION

AT THE AMERICAN ART GALLERIES

MADISON SQUARE SOUTH

From January 25th until date of sale, inclusive

THE SALE WILL BE CONDUCTED BY THOMAS E. KIRBY

NEW YORK
THE AMERICAN ART ASSOCIATION, Managers
1898

COPYRIGHT, 1898, BY
THE AMERICAN ART ASSOCIATION, NEW YORK
[ALL RIGHTS RESERVED]

COMPILED AND EDITED BY THOMAS E. KIRBY

MONOGRAPHS BY WESLEY REID DAVIS   CATALOGUE RAISONNÉ BY ARTHUR HOEBER

CONDITIONS OF SALE

1. The highest Bidder to be the Buyer, and if any dispute arise between two or more Bidders, the Lot so in dispute shall be immediately put up again and re-sold.

2. The Purchasers to give their names and addresses, and to pay down a cash deposit, or the whole of the Purchase-money, if required, in default of which the Lot or Lots so purchased to be immediately put up again and re-sold.

3. The Lots to be taken away at the Buyer's Expense and Risk upon the conclusion of the Sale, and the remainder of the Purchase-money to be absolutely paid, or otherwise settled for to the satisfaction of the Auctioneer and Managers, on or before delivery; in default of which the undersigned will not hold themselves responsible if the Lots be lost, stolen, damaged, or destroyed, but they will be left at the sole risk of the Purchaser.

4. The sale of any Article is not to be set aside on account of any error in the description, or imperfection. All articles are exposed for Public Exhibition one or more days, and are sold just as they are, without recourse.

5. To prevent inaccuracy in delivery and inconvenience in the settlement of the Purchases, no Lot can, on any account, be removed during the Sale.

6. Upon failure to comply with the above conditions, the money deposited in part payment shall be forfeited; all Lots uncleared within twenty-four hours from conclusion of Sale shall be re-sold by public or private Sale, without further notice, and the deficiency (if any) attending such re-sale shall be made good by the defaulter at this Sale, together with all charges attending the same. This Condition is without prejudice to the right of the Auctioneer or Managers to enforce the contract made at this Sale, without such re-sale, if they think fit.

THE AMERICAN ART ASSOCIATION,
Managers.

THOMAS E. KIRBY,
Auctioneer.

ORDERS TO PURCHASE

The undersigned will attend to orders to purchase at this sale:

Messrs. M. Knoedler & Co., 355 Fifth Avenue

Hermann Schaus, 204 Fifth Avenue

Messrs. Cottier & Co., 3 East Thirty-fourth Street

Messrs. Boussod, Valadon & Co., 303 Fifth Avenue

L. Crist Delmonico, 166 Fifth Avenue

M. Durand-Ruel, 389 Fifth Avenue

T. J. Blakeslee, 353 Fifth Avenue

Messrs. Arthur Tooth & Sons, 299 Fifth Avenue

Messrs. Ortgies & Co., 368 Fifth Avenue

S. P. Avery, Jr., 368 Fifth Avenue

William Macbeth, 237 Fifth Avenue

C. W. Kraushaar, 1257 Broadway

Messrs. Ainslie Brothers, 58 Wall Street

M. L. Montaignac, 9 Rue Caumartin, Paris

A Few Notes on the Works of Fortuny Included in the Collection of the late W. H. Stewart

In 1869, when Fortuny went to Paris, he took with him two half-completed works—"La Vicaria" and "Le Choix du Modèle."

"La Vicaria," which was the more advanced of the two, was finished first, and achieved so great a success that it was sold for a sum which no modern painting had ever brought, up to that time.

Some years ago Mrs. Cornelius Vanderbilt sat to me for her portrait, and Mr. Vanderbilt requested me to try to obtain "La Vicaria" from the Marquise de Carcano (who was then and is still the owner of this masterpiece), and to offer for it 250,000 francs. The Marquise, being especially fond of the magnificent picture, did not wish to part with it, and would not accept my offer. Some time after this, M. Georges Petit tried to buy the picture, but with no better success, although he offered 500,000 francs.

Mr. Stewart always regretted that he had not been able to secure this fine work, and it was he who commissioned Fortuny to paint "Le Choix du Modèle." A few years later the master enriched the fine arts by this veritable gem: Although the picture was finished in Rome, part of it was painted in Paris. I remember one night at the Palais-Royal Theatre, where we were spending the evening, Fortuny, who was a keen observer, was particularly struck by the appearance of Lhéritier, the actor. Upon his return home he bestowed upon the figure in the canvas—that stands, with snuff-box in hand, in the group that is looking at the model—the features of the comedian who had attracted his attention. This picture met with the greatest success. When Couture went to see it he was amazed, and in a very Interesting letter written to Mr. Stewart made it the subject of the highest praise. He expressed regret that Fortuny had not yet painted a picture which he had ordered from him.

Another very remarkable canvas in the collection is a study of Meissonier. I cannot pass over in silence the following anecdote:

For one of the figures in "La Vicaria" Fortuny needed a model who had the characteristic legs of a horseman. He was speaking of it to Meissonier, who said suddenly: "A horseman? Why . . . me!" Thus the great painter served Fortuny as a model, astonished and bewildered at the same time, at the rapidity with which he made the sketch. Upon his return from Poissy Fortuny confided to me that in order not to abuse the good nature of Meissonier he had not worked on the head as he would have liked to, but contented himself by completely finishing the legs !

Fortuny could not bear the sight of death. During a trip which we took together to Seville, I found it impossible to make him look at the ideally perfect head of a young Andalusian, whose body, following the custom of the country, was exposed in a glass coffin. And when M. Castillo lost his daughter, Fortuny gave the deepest proof of his affection to his friend by painting a portrait of the dead girl. Owing to reverses of fortune, this portrait found its way into the collection of Mr. Stewart.

"Fantasia Arabe," also to be found in the collection, was the first picture purchased by this keen connoisseur. Then came "L'Antiquaire," to which Fortuny added some finishing touches after his trip to Paris in 1869. What was the surprise of Mr. Stewart, to perceive in the background of the picture a portrait of himself, that Fortuny had made from a photograph. It is said that whenever his friends asked why he did not have his portrait painted he would reply that he already had one, an admirable likeness, painted by Fortuny.

It was in London in 1871 that Mr. Stewart increased his collection by buying "Le Déjeuner" and "L'Arquebusier"—two paintings, in payment of which he gave M. Goupil, in addition to a certain sum of money, a small portrait of Meissonier on horseback, painted by himself. The background of this picture was painted at Antibes.

I was speaking one day to Mr. Stewart of a fine study of a negro's head which Fortuny had in his studio in Rome, and upon his expressing a desire to own it, I wrote to Fortuny, who sent it immediately, begging Mr. Stewart to accept it as a token of his esteem. This head is the only one of the kind that the famous artist made in the same dimensions.

After Fortuny's death Mr. Stewart bought—with the idea that I would add several figures—the unfinished picture, "L'Etang de l'Alhambra," which remained in my studio for some time without my being able to decide what to add to it, finally coming to the conclusion that it was best to leave the work as it came from the hand of Fortuny.

Great was the enthusiasm produced in Paris by these water colors, which revived and gave a new lease of life to this style of painting. It was then, having achieved success in this line, that Leloir, Vibert, Worms and others, formed the Society of French Water Colorists.

My object here being only to mention a few incidents which I believe to be of some interest, I do not speak of the marvellous and original character of these water colors, the reputation of which is universally known.

"La Rue de Tanger" is a water color which was presented by the artist to Mr. Stewart, who went all the way to Rome expressly to see him.

"Le Kief," a water-color sketch of an Arabian scimeter, was painted under the following circumstances : Fortuny was in Madrid, on the eve of starting for Rome. An antiquary, anxious to possess one of the artist's works, and knowing the way to tempt him, placed before his eyes a magnificent sword-hilt of the period of the Renaissance. Fortuny, with wonderful rapidity, executed the water color, which he gave to the antiquary in exchange for the superb hilt which he coveted.

"Le Maure de Tanger" was sold to Mr. Stewart by the well-known sculptor d'Epinay, who always regretted parting with this water color, as he was never able to procure another of equal importance by the master.

Another magnificent picture, "Le Carneval," was painted in Madrid, and presented to the director of the Opéra-Comique in acknowledgment of a box which he had graciously placed at our disposal during our sojourn of six months in Spain. It passed from owner to owner, finally coming to augment the collection of Mr. Stewart.

A beautiful water color, representing an old beggar of the Roman Campagna, was exhibited at Durand-Ruel's, in Paris. Saintin, the artist, well known in New York, informed Mr. Stewart of the fact, and he bought it at once.

To finish, I will add that at the sale of the works of Fortuny, which was held in Paris, I met a number of collectors and distinguished artists, such as Couture, Dumas, M. d'Errazu, etc.—all anxious to obtain a souvenir of the master.

It was at this sale that Mr. Stewart bought "La Cour des Cochons," "L'Alberca de l'Alhambra," "Le Boucher Arabe," and "Un Paysage."

Neuville offered a sum much too large for an artist's purse for a sketch, and was extremely disappointed when it was knocked down to a higher bidder.

The eminent artist, Gérôme, made several bids for the "Musiciens Arabes," a picture which he was very anxious to own; but he did not succeed; it remained in the possession of Mrs. Fortuny, who wished to keep it.

Speaking to me of Fortuny, Gérôme said among other things: "How well he drew! There was genius in his touch!" And he advised his pupils of the École des Beaux-Arts to visit the posthumous exhibition of the great painter.

Mr. Stewart was a connoisseur of extraordinary ability. He had naturally fine taste, but in addition he trained it to such a point that his judgment was almost infallible as regards work. As he knew the artists of the present time personally, he studied their methods. He discussed art with them. He knew their theories, and was thoroughly familiar with all the various modern schools. The result was naturally shown in the paintings he collected, for they include, in addition to the marvellous Fortunys, some of the most remarkable examples of modern art by famous French, Spanish, English, German and Italian painters.

R. DE MADRAZO.

MONOGRAPHS UPON ARTISTS REPRESENTED

MONOGRAPHS

LAURENZ ALMA-TADEMA

ON a cloudless morning, the eighth of January, 1836, in a small village of Dutch Friesland, Alma-Tadema saw his mother's face and the sun. His family name was of ancient renown and is to be found among the archives that tell of the Zuyder Zee. The prefix Alma he received from his godfather, and has always used it. The early years of his life were passed under conditions of frail health and strong antagonisms to his craving to be an artist. When physicians finally declared that he would never reach his majority on account of consumptive tendencies, he was permitted to fill the brief years allotted as he pleased. So soon as vent was given to aspiration, vigor returned and the disease was conquered. He studied in the Gymnasium of Leeuwarden, and entered the Antwerp Academy in 1852. At an early date he acknowledged himself a pupil of Baron Henry Leys. His first passion was for the Merovingian barbarians, whose picturesque forms, massed against backgrounds of splendid tone, drew and held his heart. He advanced through the Nile valley, touched by all the dreaming memories of Egypt, to the land of Pallas, and later to the imperial city of the Tiber. In 1870 he fixed his residence in London. Although a quarter of a century has passed since he received letters of naturalization from his Queen, although England knows no more loyal son, he has really never ceased to be a citizen of Athens and Rome. From the start his sympathies were with the civilizations and peculiar traits of Latin and Hellenic races. The production that challenged wide interest and unlatched for him the gate to a triumphant career was "Queen Clotilda, Wife of Clovis, First Christian King of France, Instructing her Children in Arms." This painting was secured by the Antwerp Society for the Encouragement of Fine Arts, from whom it was purchased by the King of the Belgians. At the dispersion of his majesty's collection it was brought to the United

PAUL BAUDRY

THE name of this artist has large and luminous exploitation in the foyer of the Grand Opera House of Paris, the walls of which he painted between the years 1866 and 1874. There was an enforced hiatus on account of the Franco-Prussian war. This series of compositions vividly recalls that period of Renaissance frescoes which made glorious the palaces of Venice. The boldness of the designs, the poise of their treatment, fraught with a harmony of coloration unsurpassed, turn these five hundred square meters into fields of immortal legend. The beginnings of such a man have a peculiar charm. His father, a peasant of sturdy life, early took him on long walks, which generated a love of nature. He never lost the clear-eyed vision born through these journeys. The pedantry of teachers, the mechanical methods of conventional schools could not cloud it. Wherever his touch falls there is the positive accent of form and the articulation of life. His portraits group easily with the finest of the modern school. He has succeeded in varying his backgrounds as no other artist. His faces are histories. The most notable are: "Baron Jard de Panvillier," "Count Foucher de Careil," "M. Guizot," "Mme. Bernstein and her Son," "Ambroise Baudry," "M. About," "Charles Garnier," "Mme. Cezard, of Nantes," "Mlle. Deniere," and "General Count Palikao" in a landscape of battle. His "Vision of St. Hubert," to be seen on the chimney front of the grand salon in the Château of Chantilly, astonished the critics. Of this Charles Ephrussi says: "Some have determined to see in it a learned whimsicalness, others a challenge to sanctioned and necessary traditions of composition. They were accustomed to the everlasting patron of huntsmen piously kneeling before the miraculous cross. Here, in a wintry landscape lit up by sunlight without shadows, we find him under the features of the Duke de Chartres, like a primitive Capet, dressed in the Byzantine style, seen suddenly arrested, in all the ardor of desperate pursuit, before the white and luminous stag, erect on the summit of the hills, raising its head to the sky. In an assembly of figures, animals, forest trees, and hunting implements of singular but scrupulous archæology, a page, under the sympathetic features of the young Duke d'Orleans, holds a horse, whilst the pack of hounds are restless, not petrified by the miraculous apparition, but yelping and howling." He sent to the Salon of 1883 three pictures that have since become permanent pleasures to the popular heart—"La Verita," "Eve," "The Virgin, Jesus, and Saint John." In the first exhibition of the Rue de Sèze appeared "The Wave and the Pearl." A blue billow crested with foam has tossed upon the sand a nude figure of a beautiful maiden, who is lying on her side, with her back to the spectator, and turning her face with wondering eyes to look and smile at the world. This child of the sea, flung from a wave's bosom, lies on the sunny beach, in the midst of mosses and tinted shells, an incarnate, stainless joy.

Baudry was born at La Roche-sur-Yon-Vendée, November 7, 1828 ; was the pupil at La Roche of Sartoris and in Paris of Drölling. He won the *Grand Prix de Rome* in 1850 by his "Zenobia Discovered on the Banks of the Araxes." Exhibited in Salon 1857. Medals : first class, 1857, 1861-1881 ; Legion of Honor, 1861 ; Officer, 1869 ; Commander, 1875 ; Member of Institute, 1870. His rank is not only among the lordly masters of the sixteenth century, in that golden age of decorative art, but is assured in the midst of those immortals who have made resplendent the closing years of the nineteenth. M. Paul Baudry died at Paris, January 17, 1886, from a stroke of apoplexy.

JOSEPH LOUIS HIPPOLYTE BELLANGÉ

BORN in Paris February 16, 1800, and died there April 10, 1866. He was a pupil of Gros and the École des Beaux Arts. He exhibited in every Salon from 1822 to 1866, and was decorated with medals: second class, in 1824 and 1855 ; Legion of Honor, 1834 ; Officer, 1861. He was Director of the Rouen Museum 1837 to 1854. His work took expression in *genre* and historical subjects. Horace Vernet was really his master, that great national painter who voiced with such dramatic clearness the common taste and mind of France as to be called "the artist of the multitude." Bellangé marks a transition from unreal battle pieces to simple episodic painting ; a free camp life and valorous deeds are his special charm. He tells his story of events with graphic truth and directness. In the galleries at Versailles he is represented by the battles of Wagram, Loano, and Altenkirche (1837-39), with an incident from the retreat from Russia (1851). At the Leipsic Museum he has four pictures. His last and finest effort was "The Guard Dies, but does not Surrender." The "Combat in the Streets of Magenta" and "The Cuirassiers at Waterloo" were approximations to Vernet's best work.

JOSÉ BENLLIURE

THIS artist stands in the forefront of the Spanish colony at Rome, combining in himself the gifts of sculptor and painter. These are so evenly poised that it is a problem to decide in which field he excels; chisel and brush alike are wielded with equal success. He was born in Valencia in 1858. As a pupil of Domingo his talents matured early. He secured first honors in every competition, being gold medalist at Madrid, Dresden, and Berlin. He is one of the select circle pensioned by the Spanish government for residence in Italy, and has executed state orders for the decoration of public buildings.

GIOVANNI BOLDINI

MARIANO FORTUNY, under date of February 20, 1874, writes from Italy to his friend Mons. W. H. Stewart in Paris: "Don't fail to send me photographs of something good, for at Rome we are in the dark. Here they see nothing, they know nothing. I would also much like to see something by Boldini. Judging from what little I have seen, he knows what he is about." These two men were destined to develop a decided kinship in the character of the works produced by each, and many have deemed Boldini the only artist worthy to wear Fortuny's mantle. He was born at Ferrara, Italy, 1845, the son of a painter of saints. From Ferrara he went to Florence, where he remained six years. His first productions revealed scientific insight and skilled technique. Since 1872 he has lived in Paris, a pronounced type, of whom Paris is proud. The Spanish dash and swing of motive may be seen in much of his work. He is a serene optimist, in love with the warmth and glow of life. After Paris the larger number of his patrons may be found in America, where he has received generous recognition. One who has known him closely and well, defines his artistic personality in these terms: "A lover of sunlight and all the gayety and brilliancy of nature it involves, his first real successes were made with pictures in which he could give his taste in this direction fullest play. He possessed, in a rare degree, the faculty of feeling light as well as seeing it, and of painting it as he felt it, so that his sentiment might reach the spectator too. His painting of the figure, like that of the landscapes in which he was most fond of setting his groups up, was of an exquisite quality of color and ease of handling, and in the treatment of interiors his keen eye and accurate hand achieved equally felicitous results, always without the burdensome appearance of labor, from which mere superficial finish in art must suffer. No artist of his nation and century has, perhaps, come nearer to reviving in our day the essential elegance of art in France in the last century, when the broad path to the destruction of dynasties in a gulf of blood was made beautiful by the utmost refinement of genius with pen and brush."

As a painter of portraits, Boldini commands the noblest constituency. Among these that of Verdi is perhaps most eminently characteristic. On this work the art-writer Royal Cortissoz comments :

"Drawn from the life in a few hours, it has all of Boldini's best qualities concentrated and intensified. Nervous, dispassionate, scorning idealization, and rendering with the keenest precision every trait revealed by the composer's physiognomy, it has the vividness of life with a distinction that only art can give to life. The style of the portrait, the technical brilliancy, the fire and force, are incomparable. There is no portrait painter living who could help envying Boldini the grasp and authority expressed in this work. It is a model of splendid workmanship splendidly applied."

LÉON BONNAT

LÉON BONNAT was born at Bayonne, France, in 1833. When he was fourteen years old he sought Federico de Madrazo and solicited the honor of being among his pupils. This master admonished him of the arduous way and multiplied defeats confronting a young artist. Bonnat responded : "So be it, but I want to be a painter." He entered upon his career with ardor and patience. Not content with his conventional routine in the atelier, he commenced studies in the fields. One day he exhibited to Madrazo a picture he had painted secretly. The master was surprised and fascinated. Cordially embracing him, he said : " You, my boy, will make your way." He was recalled from Madrid to Paris by a death in his family. In Paris he placed himself under the tuition of Léon Cogniet, who was wise enough to leave uncurbed his natural bent. In 1857 the citizens of Bayonne furnished funds for his residence in Rome, where he tarried four years. His first successes were with small Italian pictures of unusual charm. These preluded his religious themes, in which he has won wide renown. He commanded attention by his "Adam and Eve Finding the Body of Abel," which was bought for the gallery at Lille. In 1869 his "Assumption of the Virgin" gained universal praise, and determined his drift to themes of similar character. His years at Madrid had opened on his heart the dim spiritual majesty of the old cathedrals, where he was unconsciously trained for this vocation. It has been said that the Scriptures have found in him a naturalistic commentator. He has been reproached with realism because of the scientific precision of his methods. This charge is logically true and openly a commendation of his work. His "Jacob Wrestling with the Angel" and "Christ" are the output of the world's longing to-day for truth, and lose nothing, but rather gain immeasurably, on account of taking such substance and form as the humanity of the present tense can grasp and hold. "In him," says M. Gautier, "the historical painter differs totally from the *genre* painter. As the *genre* painter showed himself fine and delicate, in the same degree the historical painter shows himself vigorous and strong." He has treated portraits with undisputed superiority, giving us a series of faces that must form a precious gallery for posterity. Here will be found such distinguished personages as "Thiers," Salon of 1877; "The Count Montalivet," Salon of 1878; "Victor Hugo," Salon of 1879; "M. Grevy," Salon of 1880; "Léon Cogniet," his second master, Salon of 1881; "Puvis de Chavannes," Salon of 1882; "Mr. Levi P. Morton," Minister Plenipotentiary of the United States, Salon, 1883. Bergerat's *Critique* upon his portrait of Victor Hugo says: "I do not know how any other painter than Bonnat would have come off from the severe and powerful theme that the august visage of the greatest poet of modern times offers. Here are no seductive accessories, no brilliant stuffs, nothing that could lighten the agony of an artist's soul, face to face with tangible, visible genius. Bonnat was sufficiently strong to undertake such a task, but what a stake he played for! for this time it was not before the public, but before immortality that he placed his easel. In art Bonnat is intrepid; he accepted his work in its formidable simplicity. Victor Hugo in a black frock coat, seated in an armchair, looking steadily in front of him. Those who have had the not-to-be-forgotten honor of being admitted to the poet's intimacy well know that black, profound glance that shines inwardly. It is the look of him who sees beyond the present. How Léon Bonnat has seized it, I do not know, but it will be an eternal glory to him. What eulogy can one address to the artist who has been able to remain a master before such a master?"

His portrait by himself reproduces his bronzed virile face with the flaming glance that astonished Federico Madrazo and that sparkles brighter than ever under the shade of his arched eyebrows. His honors have had significant progression— second *Grand Prix de Rome*, 1858; medal of honor, 1869; medals: second class,

1861-'63, '69 ; Legion of Honor, 1867 ; Officer, 1874 ; Commander, 1882 ; Member of Institute of France and Knight of the Order of Leopold. His portraitures of women and children are full of truthful sentiment and delicate observation. They are well within the realm of the beautiful without falling to the level of prettiness.

Léon Bonnat stands for the conjunction between French modern painting and the old Spanish schools. He has poured the fresh blood of naturalism into the one, and a serene reserve, a chastened passion, into the other.

RICHARD PARKES BONINGTON

ALTHOUGH English by parentage and birth, Richard Parkes Bonington is claimed by France. He was born in the village of Arnold, near Nottingham, on the 25th of October, 1801, and died in London September 23, 1828. His father was an artist of moderate equipment, doing reasonable things in portraiture and landscape. Having exhausted his resources in England, he took his family to Paris, where his son studied in the Louvre, and later under the guidance of Baron Gros. Eugène Delacroix, swift always to recognize young men of mark, gave him fellowship and unqualified praise. His water colors sold rapidly, showing landscape and river views, especially exploiting the Seine and street scenes in the older sections of Paris. His figure-work was fine, and when introduced into his themes gave increased force. He won the gold medal of 1824, and shortly after visited Italy, where he executed elaborate Venetian studies. It was in the exhibition of these that his wider reputation was made. It was a sorrow to Bonington that England remained so long ignorant of her son. Two years before his decease recognition came through the exhibition of two of his pictures in London, when he was favorably mentioned as "an unknown but promising artist." It was somewhat of a comfort that for ten years Parisians had literally contended for the privilege of purchasing from his easel. The seal of death was set on him by the hot sun while painting out-of-doors. He caught a fever which developed into hasty consumption. He sought medical skill and rest in England, but his splendid physique had been undermined, and he passed hence, in the home of a friend, after a confining illness of three weeks. Sir Thomas Lawrence, writing of Bonington's demise, said: "I have never known in my own time an early death of talent so promising, so rapidly and obviously improving." Bonington produced a number of lithographs, which are to-day greatly treasured by collectors. His painting, "François et la Duchesse d'Etampes," is in the Louvre.

LÉON BONVIN

AS the poet in the realm of words is the real and complete artist; as his metrical setting enables him to show a part as well as a whole, to make perfect the smallest thing, to give beauty and immortality to an emotion, an image,

> "As when the dawn glows o'er the glowing deep,
> And sea and sky are but asunder as a two-leaved book
> All of one story,"

which may not be expanded beyond the dozen lines of a sonnet—so Bonvin has, in contrast to the prosing artists of his time, caught the sonnet spirit for his themes. This is the more marvelous when we recall that he had no quiet retreat or chosen tower in which to open his note-book, but kept a wayside inn. He had only the chill hours of the morning or the weary ones of the night, when, for a brief space, he was free from the bitter railings of a wife (who faithfully misunderstood him), in which to make his studies and paint his water colors.

He was born at Vaugirard, within the environs of Paris, on February 28, 1834. His father had been in turn a servant, a barber, a soldier, and a gendarme. His last avocation was that of a rural policeman, with the privilege of selling drink. The old man, it is said, though virtuous, was ferociously selfish. He would not allow his sons to be apprenticed to a trade, but kept them home to act as waiters. Léon, the youngest of four brothers, was buffeted from childhood. He was large-boned, of heavy build, awkward, and apparently clumsy-handed. Beneath this coarse vesture there were fibres as delicate as those of a sensitive child, nerve-lines that trembled in the breath of flowers, tuneful chords more easily touched than those of an Æolian harp. He devoted himself to water colors. His brother François, who early ran away from home to become, in due time, a painter of pronounced power, saw in his rough chrysalis the folded wings, and sent him to the school in the Rue de l'École de Medicine, founded in the eighteenth century by Bachelier. In 1861 he married, and was thereafter perpetually reminded of the harness he had put on. Through pictures painted by him we are familiar with the interior of his house, which had been built out of materials given him by contractors in part payment for his keeping of their accounts, on the day when they came to eat at his tavern and to settle with their factors. He had learned music from an old German who lived near by, and played with discriminating taste. Beethoven was his favorite; Gluck often relieved his silence and sorrow. There was a room just above the bar, where he had placed a harmonium, bought after years of patient saving of small sums paid him as *pourboires*. His wife, an ignorant, scoffing creature, would suddenly rush up the stairs, tap him on the shoulder, and say : " Léon, you are boring the people down below with your gloomy church music. Play them something gay." He would respond by melodies which the street organs had brought into fashion, and thus lose the enchantment of his heart under the spell of the great tone masters. He was in the habit of painting early in the day, before customers arrived for their draught of white wine. At night he would work under the light of a lamp inclosed in a box, which flung a broad radiation upon the flowers which he had gathered. In a thoughtful review of his individuality as an artist another has said :

"Those who have tried with sincerity to paint flowers in the open air have felt how difficult it is to combine accessories with them ; either their brilliancy must be subordinated to the landscape, or the landscape must be sacrificed. Léon Bonvin has succeeded in accomplishing the alliance with a talent all the more sure because it is simple and without artifice. Here we have a family of goldfinches that have alighted on the dry branches of some thistles and wild aniseed ; the vermilion of their beaks, the black of their cowls, the chrome of their wings, animate with sparks of brightness the opal gray of the fog through which the sun is penetrating. There we have a chrysanthemum which has grown up vigorously on a heap of rubbish, and glories in its starry flowers with their sulphur-yellow centres, while in the successive planes of the morning mist one sees a man digging, the profiles of the edge of a village and of the church steeples. (See the aquarelle entitled 'The Market-Garden.') Here, again, is a fuller's thistle with its silhouette of threatening prickles, some wild carrots, and grasses shooting up in tender tubes ; their outlines strike across a sky of light, drifting vapors ; the light of the horizon is broken by the glacis of the fort of Issy, and by the outstretched arms of a windmill. Another water color is an evening effect of boundless melancholy. We might believe ourselves in a cemetery assisting at some tragic and distant conflagration which is flinging its sad smoke in the air. Through the knolled branches, which are losing their leaves, a woman is seen passing, bent beneath a burden, and hastening toward a cold-looking and cheerless dwelling-house."

These four water colors belong to the collection of the late Mr. W. T. Walters, of Baltimore, who bought them of the artist. Mr. Walters possessed more than fifty examples of Bonvin's genius. Twenty are landscapes combined with flowers, ten are landscapes alone, fifteen are subjects of flowers, and ten are studies of fruit. He could image an apple bough in blossom so freshly that its perfume would seem to fill the nostrils. Bonvin had no interest for plants that were prisoners ; hothouse growths were without a voice to him. When asked by Mr. Walters whether he had not a desire to paint cultivated flowers he answered: "Do not ask me to do these; my heart is not in them." A half-witted daisy by the roadside lifted a friendly face to his own, while the grasses and gorse of the fields were for him the motives and messengers of Heaven's kindness to earth. It was pitiful beyond words that this rare-natured man was left to fight in solitude his hard battle with misery and want. Friends have since read in his work premonitions of the hopeless struggle and blind despair. "I have seen in the collection of Mr. Lucas," writes one, "a picture which answers to the impressions of his aching soul: beyond a foreground of buttercups, wild roses, and brambles stretch a landscape darkened by the approach of a storm; some fields, where a few stunted trees are growing; a pool of water, in which is reflected a bit of dim blue sky; some hills quite near, that give one the sensation of a closed life. Generally, and even nearly always, the signature of Léon Bonvin is traced neatly in black; in this case it is written in somber red. This signature is followed by the date, 1865.

"The winter of 1865 was terrible for Léon Bonvin. Other taverns had been opened in the neighborhood as the new houses advanced over the plain. The workmen had perhaps felt embarrassed at coming into contact with artists and *bourgeois*, and they no longer came. Léon Bonvin, having nothing to do at home, had even worked as a carter with the stone wagons. Debts were accumulating. He had a bill of thirteen hundred francs to meet. He was tortured by jealousy. His heart and his hands were torn by every thorn.

"On January 29, 1866, he went to return some ancient glass which had been obligingly lent to him; thence to see a dealer in water colors, who did not deign to choose anything out of his portfolio. He found all the water colors 'too dark, not gay enough.'

"A week afterward M. François Bonvin addressed the following letter to M. Albert' de la Fizelière, who, a few weeks before, had called attention to the misery of the artist.

"'MY DEAR SIR: Here is a very sad conclusion for your article in the *Evénement* of the 13th November last. My poor brother, in spite of all his efforts, has been overcome by evil fortune. The attempts which he made a week ago to sell the last drawings he had executed were vain. The picture-dealer ——— offered him ten francs for drawings for which the others ordinarily paid him sixty francs.

"'The future seemed to him more gloomy than the past. Instead of confiding to me the full extent of his needs, he determined to have done with everything, and he went and hung himself on a tree in the wood of Meudon on the evening of January 31. You knew him, and you know that fraternity does not blind me when I proclaim that he was indeed the best and purest of the best. As an artist, one has only to look at his drawings to recognize his worth. His musical aptitudes were unknown.

"'All this is dead!

"'Now there remain three children and a weakly wife, and I myself, who am almost in as great misery, for at the present moment all the fruit that I have gathered of my labors is to have but few debts relatively to what I should have had if I had allowed myself all the necessaries of life. We need, then, dear sir, your kind aid to endeavor to organize a sale. For my part, I have never failed to respond to the appeals that have been made to me by others in similar circumstances, and I hope I shall find amongst our colleagues enough sympathy to help me in the sad mission which has fallen to my lot.

"'F. BONVIN.

"'6th of January, 1860.

"'P.S.—His body was not found until Saturday, at Meudon, at the foot of a tree, near the pond of Villebois. The branch had broken. This is the only damage he ever did in his life. He was just thirty-two years of age.'"

A broken branch in a forest, unconsciously broken; the only damage he ever did in his life. The Church buried him in unconsecrated ground, forgetting that from a child he had read the gospels of God's blossoms, and had pondered the hour-book of Nature as a breviary for meditation and prayer.

Could birds and flowers have held convocation over the cold clay, they might have said: "Let us put him beneath a coverlid of moss in the stillest spot of Meudon wood, and tell the frail violets he loved to grow there always for his memory."

"CHAM"

(Nom de plume)

THE Count Amédée Charles Henri de Noé was born January 20, 1819, on a small island near Mirande, whence the name of the family is derived, whose nobility dates from the Carlovingian kings. He studied under Paul Delaroche, Charlet, and Launy. As Ham was the second son and scapegrace of Noah, so "Cham," or Ham, was the second son and scapegrace of Jude Amédée Compte de Noé, a peer of France. His mother was an English lady. He was a great wit, and the political caricaturist of *Charivari* (the French *Punch*). The count was one of the founders of the Republic in 1875. The blending of two strains of blood in his veins combined the most striking characteristics of the two nations. His satiric force was sweeping and yet concise. Paris afforded rich soil and hot incongruities for his ranging pencil. The downfall of the Empire, the incoming of the Republic, with its communistic tendencies, brought about the very complications in which the caricaturist delights. "Cham" was the largest figure in his day in the school of satire, and was openly recognized as the successor to Gavarni, than which higher praise cannot be spoken. He died in the year 1879. Only a few of his productions bear the family name; they generally show his pseudonym, "Cham."

PAUL JEAN CLAYS

THIS distinguished Belgian was born at Bruges, 1819. He was the pupil of Gudin, in Paris, devoting himself to *genre* marine subjects, breaking the traditions of the average artist, who spasmodically surges over his canvas with great storms. Clays was Wordsworthian in his work, revealing the waters asleep or stirred by the tide's pulses. His studies on the birth of waves under the caress of the breeze; the uneasy shivers that have a menace of the winds in them; the clearness of rivers widening to the sea; the snapping reflections of the sun's rays crossing the faint crests that shimmer on the bosom of the Scheldt; the cool tones and humid greys of the skies of western Flanders; these are the *motifs* that allure his hand. He settled at Brussels, where, in 1851, he received the gold medal. At the Salon of 1877 he exhibited "The Zuyder Zee" and "A Canal in Zealand." His later works show travel beyond the girdle of his moist horizons—views on the Thames and of the North Sea. In these he still held to his mood of serenity. "The magical charm of morning, the golden brilliancy of the evening twilight, the infinite variety of tones which light produces on waves, became the ideal of the sea painters after Clays." Like him, they scarcely left the shore, or, at least, when taking the track of the high seas, kept a blue line of hills on the horizon.

JOSEPH THÉODORE COOSEMANS

WE recognize in the name of this artist one of the most interesting landscape painters of Europe. His studio is in Brussels, where he has been honored with the Order of Leopold. Among his impressive works may be numbered "Entrance to Gorge aux loups in Fontainebleau Forest" (Exposition Universelle, Amsterdam, 1883), "Road in Heath of Geuck Plateau Belle Croix at Fontainebleau" (Munich Exhibition, 1883), "Autumn Landscape" (Jubilee Exhibition, Berlin, 1886). He has by sheer force of perception and exactness of knowledge put before us examples of strong feeling. The two landscapes in this collection indicate that he went straight to nature. Few winter scenes run so perfectly the entire gamut of cold notes and with such simplicity of expression.

JEAN BAPTISTE CAMILLE COROT

THIS distinguished landscape painter was born in Paris, July 20, 1796; he died there February 23, 1875. He was the pupil of Michallon and of Victor Bertin. These taught him little. He says that, having passed two winters with Bertin when he arrived in Rome, he was the merest tyro at sketching. "Two men stopped to converse; I began to sketch them, beginning on one part—the head, for example. They would separate, leaving me with a couple of pieces of their heads on my paper. I saw some children on the steps of a church; no sooner did I begin to sketch than their mother called them. I saw that in this way my portfolio would be filled with ends of noses, foreheads, and locks of hair. I resolved not to return, when I went out to sketch, without having something in its entirety. I attempted, therefore, to sketch, in the twinkling of an eye, the first group that presented itself: if the figures remained in position for a time, I had at least the character—the general outline; if they remained long, I added details. I practiced in this way until I was able to fix the outlines of a ballet at the opera, with a few strokes made with lightning-like celerity." This habit came to the front when he wrestled breast to breast with Nature, applying himself not so much to the form and line as to the life. In the clear-eyed, sympathetic study which M. Albert Wolff has given to his work, we find these words: "The controlling principle in this great artist is never to strike the Philistine by panoramic magnitude, but to establish in his art the vibration which is in Nature, to take by surprise its perpetual life, to send the air circulating through space, to shake the foliage in the breeze. He wishes to disengage and carry to his canvas the poet's impression of the object. This poetry, he rightly deems, is not only in the composition—the composition is to him of small account—it is in the truth, for nothing is of such finished poetry as truth itself. Whether it be the old bridge of Mantes, glimpsed through the tall trees which reflect themselves in the sunny waters, or Garda Lake, stretching out of sight into the light of dawn, with the leafage of the trees upon its brink trembling in the wind—it is always the country feeling which this artist applies to his canvas, whatever the aspect. Corot is the excelling interpreter of the serenity of Nature.

"We need not be surprised that a style, springing, as it may be said, all fresh from the nerves of a primitive artist who sought the support of no predecessor, was so long a subject of debate. The public had been so habituated to see filing before its eyes a succession of rigid landscapes that it was naturally troubled before the vibrating themes of Corot. Those who recommence eternally the official teaching of the schools rejected him desperately. And he, the quiet, inspired man, heard little of the clamor in the solitude of his woods, on the banks of the pool, where he opened his soul to the enchantment of creation."

Corot has opened to us the strong tenderness of Nature's heart. He remembered that from of old the pillars of Hiram were crowned with lilies; that the mountain wall must carry its frieze of mosses, the forest its fringe of ferns. He has the mood of Hellenic calm, and is a Greek in the joyous accord which he feels with the rhythmic pulse of the universe. He has, as no other, found the secret of massing tree-forms and foliage on trees, which makes the leaf type the tree and the tree the leaf. A gigantic oak is lifted against the sky, in the two color tones of a single banner on its boughs, showing the misty green of the up side and grey of the down side. This scientific glance and grasp is suggestive of the whole range of Corot's realism, which is interpenetrated with dreams of the ideal. He has helped the world to breathe and feel its atmosphere. Breadth of view is on the vision of those who sit at his feet. He is the herald of the gentle dawn; the evangelist of the evening fields. "But he is monotonous," says the critic—"grey, always grey." "To thoroughly appreciate my landscapes," said Corot, "it is at least necessary to have patience, to let the fog clear up. They are not easily understood, but when they are understood they ought to please." His verdure and sunlight may seem to drift past us as under a veil, but on the farther side every object retains its relative value. The Divine Limnist works behind half-translucent curtains. The heavens have their azure of mystery,

"And store the dew in their deeps of blue,
Which the fires of the sun come *tempered* through."

France paid to Corot the signal honor of an exhibition of his works in the Melpomene, the grand hall of the École des Beaux Arts. Two hundred of his canvases occupied the walls where Baudry's masterpieces won their unanticipated triumph. In 1833 he received a second-class medal; two of the first class came to him in 1848 and 1855. In 1846 he received the Legion of Honor, and was made an Officer in 1867. A little while before his head was pillowed in final rest, the artists, independent of the official partisans of exhibitions, held a meeting, and offered Father Corot a gold medal. With radiant heartiness he thanked those whom he called his children. He had the privilege of never growing old; his life was a perpetual artistic renovation.

"When young he had strolled singing over the plains; advanced years found him just as free from care as he had been half a century before. We discovered him bent like a schoolboy over his themes to the last, now erasing with a movement of anger the study which would not come up to the example of nature contemplated by the artistic eye, now drawing back with sudden satisfaction to better calculate the effect of the effort; when we would hear him from far off, approving himself aloud and awarding himself a prize, with the words 'Famous, that bit!' or criticising himself roundly with the sentence, 'We will begin it all over again, my lad!'"

He passed serenely to his rest. On his final day he roused with a smile, and said: "Last night, in my dreams, I saw a landscape with a sky all rosy. It was charming, and still stands before me quite distinctly; it will be marvelous to paint." Above Ville d'Avray there lingers yet a sky of rose, like the afterglow of an Egyptian sunset, and in that sky shines the steady star of his fame.

CHARLES FRANÇOIS DAUBIGNY

AN artist who has shown to the world a fresh view of the loveliness of nature. He had in a peculiar sense his own standpoint and individual equation, which gave glimpses and opened vistas hitherto sealed. He was born in Paris in 1817, and was the youngest of the famous Barbizon circle. His antecedents were favoring forces to his chosen vocation, his father and kindred being exhibitors at the Salon. He passed his curriculum in the studio of Delaroche, and appeared, when nineteen years old, with a picture and an etching in the Salon of 1836. Through a misapprehension as to terms of competition, he lost the *Prix de Rome*. Instantly he determined to go to the imperial mother at his own charges. In company with his room-mate, named Mignan, he started on a tour to Italy. To meet the expenses of the expedition, they pinched and saved small sums, putting them in a hole punched in the wall. At the end of the year they tore down the wall and found eighteen hundred francs in their hands. Henriet, in his memoirs, narrates: "Daubigny and Mignan set out, knapsack on back, heavily shod, stick in hand, intoxicated with sunshine and liberty. They felt that all the world was their own. Their walk was one long enchantment as they saw new perspectives open every moment before their eyes and a succession of panoramas unrolled, at the richness, the accent, and the variety of which they marveled. Beyond Lyons they recognized with ecstasy the presence of the South by the intenser light of the sky and the grandeur of the landscape dressed in a vegetation unknown in our latitudes —the olive, the cypress, the pine, all the beloved trees of the antique idyl. They passed at last across the delightful garden shut in on the left by the first mountains of the Alps and on the right by the peaks of the Cévennes. At last they trod the epic soil of Italy. They visited Florence, Rome, and Naples, finally settling down to work at the old Roman resort of Subiaco."

The two friends remained in Italy a year, when again they started northward, heading for Paris, walking every foot of the distance and arriving penniless. But little trace of Italian influence can be found in the pictures of Daubigny, in which regard he distinctly differed from Corot, who absorbed with eagerness the classic charm of Italy, revealing it in his style ever after, most notably in his canvas of "Orpheus Greeting the Morn." At the age of twenty-three Daubigny attained success, and never lost it.

In 1848 he won a second-class medal, in 1853 one of the first class. The seal was set upon his reputation when the Emperor, in 1852, purchased his picture of "The Harvest" for the Tuileries, following it, in 1853, with the purchase of another for St. Cloud. In 1859 he was invested with the Legion of Honor; was made an Officer of the Order in 1875.

The picture that won him the Cross of the Legion was "Springtime." A peasant girl rides through a field of tender, upright grain; the marked features in the landscape show groups of young apple trees, whose branches quiver with blossoms. It was purchased by the government, and is now in the Louvre. Daubigny was destined to be the enchanter of the rivers of France. He built a large boat, which became his drifting studio and home. This was arranged for long trips; the cooking was done on board; there was a good wine-cellar and well-filled larders. Here he adjusted his easel and "went on the watch" for scenes. He became a familiar figure to the peasants and boatmen along the banks of the Oise, the Marne, and Seine, who grew fond of him and called him "captain," a title which gave him pleasure, as he affected, so far as his voyages would allow, to be a hardened sailor, made rugged by risky navigations.

His "Valley of the Optivoz," painted in 1853, ranks a masterpiece. Of this picture the Count Clement de Riz says: "The eye rests on every part with pleasure and floats undecided between the sapphire of the sky and the velvet of the vegetation. One seems to smell the clover and hay, to hear the hum of the insects, and catch the sparkling of the light over the wheat fields."

His "Lock of the Optivoz," exhibited in the Salon of 1855, was bought by the government, and is in the Louvre, as are also "Springtime" and the "Vintage."

In the special class of subjects to which he was drawn he was unrivaled and has found no successor. His influence on the art of the century, like sun-rays that have penetrated the earth, cannot be overestimated. Of him Albert Wolff says: "He brought to landscape painting the realistic keynote in the best sense of the term—that is to say, the matching of real objects by a deeply felt stroke, so that with each new sensation freshly breathed in the presence of Nature, he shifted his art; in one picture, where the painter has paused to smile at the perfect grace of a landscape, his painting is full of the lambent flatteries which accompany a beam of the sun in the springtime; in another, where he has found himself astounded before the grandeur of the scene, he rises to the calm height of greatest art ; when the landscape had struck him, especially by its general planes, he flung it on the canvas in those marvelous sketches which the artist refused to carry on further because he had nothing to add to this massy statement ; at other times he insinuates himself into details as exhaustively as possible and refines on his work to the utmost limits of execution. The career of Daubigny is based on the simple and truthful art theory that the handling of a picture ought to reflect the mood felt, that the painter can no more work perpetually in the same style than the writer can employ an unvarying form for the play of his thought."

When he reached the meridian of his triumphs, beset by collectors, solicited by dealers, fawned upon by Paris, he remained uncorrupted and could not be tempted like Père Corot, who, in late life, not unfrequently did hurried service to his art in the shape of small panels, which the old man was pleased to call "little dreams." Of the group to which he belonged he was perhaps nearest to Corot not only in artistic sympathy, but in tenderness of personal affection. He was therefore pained at noting his hasty work, and blamed him for it with some bitterness. Daubigny kept his heart sweet to the end. He died of a disease contracted through long exposures in his "La Bottin." The damp river shores yielded winsome shadings of mist and light, but they also surrendered rheumatisms that clutched him remorselessly, lining his clear face with pain and aging him beyond his age.

Death found him waiting without fear. As the vesture of his mortality was unclasped, his thoughts turned to those who had dropped their mantles before him, "his rivals in renown." He said between final spasms for breath: "Adieu; I am going to see up there whether friend Corot has found me any new subjects for landscape painting."

ALEXANDRE GABRIEL DECAMPS

THE picture by which Decamps entered the Salon of 1827 was that of a Turk, which, it is said, was evolved from his inner consciousness. He had not yet visited the East, but the soft fire of a thoroughbred Orientalist glowed in his blood, originally kindled, perchance, through the arteries of some far-off ancestor. Decamps was born in Paris, March 3, 1803 ; he died at Fontainebleau, August 22, 1860. He was sent, when a boy, into the country, where he ran wild ; his only companionship was that of peasants, whose *patois* he spoke, whose manners he imitated. This unrestrained period, lasting for three years, gained a strong grip on the development of his character, which was always impatient of restraint. His tastes gravitated to the unrefined side of society. Conscious of intense possibilities, he was eager to break the shell that limited them, yet unready to discipline his powers by that training and intelligence which are the impartial but arbitrary conditions of permanent success. Looking backward through misspent opportunities, he lived to grieve bitterly over the loss of that larger birthright which might have been his. Monsieur Chesneau, in the *Chefs d'École*, says of Decamps' youthful blunders : "Cruel chastisement for an hour of weakness at the decisive time ! he lived with the crushing certainty that he had not expressed what was in him ; he died with the conviction of having left his work undone." It was his ambition to rank as a great historical painter, but just here the fetter lay on his faculty ; he had not the academic training, the skill of fiber which means drill of force, the alert and technical vision which pierces the semblances of affairs and goes direct to the crimson center of life's battle. Had Decamps known, in his formative period, the tuition of a great master, there would have been absolutely no measure to the display of his magnificent equipment. Bravely facing the inner captivities which he mourned, he has wrought a marvelous series of canvases, setting the almost fierce individualism of his work on the very eye-line of the world's salon. There are critics who, differing from Decamps' judgment, feel that he has been the gainer for the lack and loss of early discipline. They say he was a predestined artist ; that his taste came without effort ; that his finest traits are found in what he did in defiance of the instruction he received ; that the heroic painters, the men of Titanic build, fail to indicate the slightest influence of their teachers. True ; but we must bear in mind that it appears a satire on the part of Providence to appoint mediocre ability to develop the children of genius. The master of Decamps was Abel de Pujol, whom Albert Wolff classifies as really somebody under the Restoration, while waiting to be nobody at all under Louis Philippe. Decamps showed a large susceptible soul to the world of events around him. Sensitively responding to these, he took control of the facts they presented, sought the environment and local color with care, and then put them out through the luminous impressions of his own intelligence. The East he dreamed of in his studio at Fontainebleau was not the East he found when, inspired by the struggle of the Greeks for independence, he hurried to Athens, his brain full of the ideals of Pericles, his heart stung with ardor in their behalf. The disenchantment was not long in coming, not only there, but afterward in Asia Minor and along the shore-lines of the Mediterranean. When he had seen and digested the Greek, the Turk, the Arab on their native soils, he returned to Paris far wiser and quite willing to break forever with those creatures that pose or stride in the average Eastern picture.

It is not a matter of wonder that after dipping his brush in the actual sunlight of the Orient he became the colorist of his time. His effort never degenerates into triviality. He paints a brace of beggars with the dignity of patriarchs, and an episode from a street corner in Cairo with the charm of an old world idyl. It has been observed that while Delacroix painted with color, Decamps painted with light. His figures are draped in the glow of the sun. He was attracted by scriptural themes, as evidenced in his "Samson" and "The Good Samaritan." Honors were welcomed, but to him appeared few and inadequate. He could not be satisfied, because unrestful before a goal unreached. He took his bread from the world, but found it a stone in his hand when he sought to feed his loftier aspirations. The loneliness, the pathos of his career irritated his heart. We read the roll of his medals —Paris, 1831-1834 ; Legion of Honor, 1839 ; Officer of the same, 1851—and are certain that to him these were but small crests for the decoration of an evening hour compared to the ideal for which his spirit thirsted.

Suddenly thrown from his horse, and violently striking a tree, he was killed in the forest of Fontainebleau.

ERNEST ANGE DUEZ

HE was born in Paris, March 8, 1843. His master in art was Carolus Duran. As *genre* painter he obtained medals—third class, 1874, and first class, 1879 ; Legion of Honor, 1880. His large religious pictures brought him his first-class medal. Subsequently he turned aside from expressions of this character and took a more varied range of subjects. He painted animals, landscapes, portraits. His representations of street and café life have fine stories, told in a firm yet delicate strain. He has kept the freshness of his early emotions and the ardor of his original enthusiasms. His career not unfittingly stands for the counsel of Leonardo da Vinci : "It is not being a strong man among painters to succeed in only one thing—the nude, the head, animals, landscapes. There is no mind so gross that in time, with continued and earnest application to one thing, it cannot succeed in accomplishing it satisfactorily. A painter should be universal, study everything he comes in contact with, render account of all that he sees, let nothing remarkable pass without keeping a sketch or reminder of it, and only cling to what is in all ways excellent."

HENRI LOUIS DUPRAY

HE was born at Sedan (Ardennes), November 3, 1841. A pupil of Pils and Léon Cogniet. Patiently seeking the path of the historical painter, he has achieved solid success, ranking with Detaille as a leader in the new school of military artists. Fine composition, correct color, and vigorous treatment are combined with a thorough perception of the war spirit and a mastery of technical details. His soldiers are not men who have come out of an enamel factory, stiff and rigidly complete, not wanting a gaiter button, but are plastic forms drilled into strength, who have been under fire and have not flinched. Medals: 1872, 1874; Legion of Honor, 1878.

FIRMAN-GIRARD

THE favorite pupil of Gleyre was born at Poncin, 1838. Under his master's suggestion he adopted a style of light *genre* subjects treated in fresh and luminous coloration. His medals were awarded—third class, 1863; second class, 1874. At the Salon of 1875 he exhibited "The Garden of the Godmother"; in 1874, "The Fiancés," a picture of unusual refinement. His "Flower Market" was a delightful epitome of Paris. The actual technique leaves nothing to be desired; every detail is elaborated with fidelity, but the amount of detail is excessive, the minutiæ overdone. While no color note is missing, the theme lacks synthesis, that texture as a whole, that breadth of light and shade which becomes the harmonic utterance of a great picture achieved by Claude Monet's "Field of Poppies." Firman-Girard achieves it in another canvas, known as "The Flower Girl," which has placed his reputation on an enduring basis. Here every value is balanced with the veritable touch of a master. The girl is a lovely outblossoming of flesh, pure, radiant, and *naïve;* the perfumed chalices she cries are but garden echoes of herself. The Stewart collection gains in this example a melodic charm not to be found elsewhere.

MARIANO FORTUNY

RÉUS is a small thrifty town in the Province of Tarragona. An event significant for the universal art world occurred at six o'clock in the morning, June 11, 1838: a man-child was born to Mariano Fortuny, a cabinetmaker, and his wife, Teresa Marsal. The waters of baptism consecrating this new pilgrim within a few hours after his advent, were administered by Juan Yxart, parish priest of the Church of St. Peter the Apostle. The child, named also Mariano Fortuny, shot prophetic flashes into the near future, and foretold in early years the career he was destined to follow. When a mere lad he lost his father and mother. He often gypsied over the country, tramping leagues to display a group of wax figures. At the age of fourteen he left Réus, accompanied by his grandfather, who was taking him a journey of sixty miles, walking every foot of the distance, to meet M. Domingo Talarn. This artist was at once fascinated by the sketches shown him. On October 3, 1853, Mariano was registered on the rolls of the Academia de Bellas Artes, of Barcelona, where he remained until the end of 1856, studying meanwhile under M. Claudio Lorenzalez. In 1855 he painted in distemper several themes of significant size based upon religious subjects. A strong impulse stirred his mind through the figure-work of Gavarni, whose influence he never ceased to feel. In November he began to fit himself for the competition for the prize of a pensioner at Rome, offered by the Provincial Council. He drew on wood, made cuts, lithographed, and etched. These variations produced little of value, but gave to eye and hand a certain subtle perception and deftness of touch which culminated in a mastery with the brush unsurpassed and rarely equaled.

Fortuny gained, by the unanimous vote of the Council, the *Prix de Rome*, March 6, 1857. His subject was "Raymond III. Nailing the Arms of Barcelona to the Castle Tower of Foix." He left for Rome March 14, 1858, and arrived five days later. One can picture this youth of twenty years confronting the garnered treasures, the serious commands, the majestic memories, the lofty ideals, the processional splendors of that imperial city. With keen discrimination and a *naïve* independence of judgment, he writes of his impressions, under date of May 3d, to his old master, M. Lorenzalez:

"What I admire above all are the frescoes of Raphael at the Vatican, particularly 'Mount Parnassus,' the 'School of Athens,' the 'Dispute on the Holy

Sacrament,' and the 'Burning of Bergo.' The other masters did not impress me as I expected. What I call a well-painted picture, and which I place above all others, is a portrait of Innocent X. by Velasquez.

"I know that it is necessary to exercise great prudence in the choice best adapted to one's talent, for, by reason of the many opportunities one has, it is as easy to retrograde as to obtain good results. I say this because I am discouraged by seeing how little it profits many among the painters, who pass entire months in these galleries, copying the great masters, and who afterwards do not know how to draw a face from memory."

It was at Rome that the powers of this child of Catalonia began to stir in their sheath, "and that," says M. Gautier, "more by the blooming of his natural gifts than by the direct influence of the great masters whom the world goes to admire and copies on its knees. Don't let us in the least blame this worship, but it is good sometimes to follow the bent of our own nature, and to see with one's own eyes."

Fortuny was susceptible to but was not enslaved by these enthroned dynasties of art set up through centuries of noble endeavor. He must take sunlight on his own retina, and his art, as he breathed the airs of the Albanian mountains, through the valves of his own life. He maintained to the last chapter of his earthly career a certain freedom of faith and valor of conviction that gave to his personality a nameless charm. After a stay of seven months he sent two pictures from his easel to M. Pedro Bover, of Réus, one showing a view of the Tiber, with the castle of St. Angelo in the distance; the other, "Nereides sur un lac," at the fringe of a forest. He designed the funds secured from the sale of these to go to his grandfather. The old man wore out his heart in yearning for the child who had been his comrade as well as his kinsman, and died on the 19th of March, 1859, just a year after his grandson arrived in Rome and as the latter was about to express to him a "Saint Mariano."

When war was declared between Spain and Morocco, the Town Council of Barcelona proposed to Fortuny to accompany the army to Africa to make studies and paint souvenirs of the campaign. He accepted their terms and left by the first steamer. He carried letters of presentation to the commander-in-chief, O'Donnell, and to Generals Ros d'Olano and Prim and a number of other eminent persons. He reached Tetuan in February in company with M. Escriu, who became later on his brother-in-law. The letters of introduction were of small account; he suffered severe hardships, going often hungry and sleeping upon the ground. On the 11th of March the battle of Samsa was fought. Fortuny pressing to the front, a ball spurted the dust at his feet. "Ah!" said a soldier, "that was meant for the painter," but the painter was intent on business and paid scant heed to danger. On the 23d the bloody conflict of Wad-Ras came on, the Spaniards gaining a decisive victory. Throughout these experiences the artist was enlarging his world, populating his brain, working incessantly, making sketches in oil and water color, figures massed and single, Arabs, soldiers, his fellow countrymen the Catalans, Jews, and landscapes. On the 23d of April he started with his friend for Madrid, which they reached at the same hour as the staff of the army of Africa. He was introduced at once by M. Augustin Rigalt to M. Federico Madrazo, who, seven years afterward, gave him his daughter Cecilia in marriage. His studies of the war were exhibited publicly in Barcelona and created general admiration. The Town Council sent an address to the governor of the province, which revealed a pride and solicitude worthy of the grandfather who was asleep in his grave at Réus.

"The painter Fortuny has happily returned from Africa, where he collected, at the cost of great danger, and with a perseverance and zeal worthy of all praise, subjects of the highest interest, which he will doubtless use in the work the Town Council has entrusted to him. Your Excellency has seen his portfolios of sketches, souvenirs, and impressions, and will understand the great effect these drawings, so simple in appearance, will one day produce. So exactly do they show us the places where our heroic army has accomplished great deeds of arms; also the dress, character, and manners of our adversaries in this African war.

"Fortuny to this time has well done his honorable task, but this is not all. In order that the young painter may finish his noble work, for the glory and honor of his country, it is necessary his genius should feed upon, strengthen itself, and grow prolific by study of the great masters. The Town Council feels that it is needful that he should visit Paris, Munich, Berlin, Brussels, Milan, and Florence, to the end that, throwing a rapid *coup d'œil* on their museums and artistic monuments, he can better reconcile with the principles of art his conceptions, as yet crude. A trip of six or eight weeks, with a companion so imbued with passion for the beauties of art, will suffice to accomplish what the Town Council proposes."

This plan was only realized in part. He studied in Paris, the Museum at Versailles, and later in that of Florence. His progress was rapid and brilliant. At Paris he frequently saw Meissonier, who was greatly drawn to him, for whom he in turn cherished the sincerest admiration, whose influence over him was one of maturing force. He painted his portrait, which afterward came into the possession of Mr. Stewart. The figure could but be fine; the pose is striking and martial, bending backward to show every line of the magnificent body, which wears a large curved sabre. By action of the Town Council Fortuny was requested to make a second visit to Africa to reimpress his mind with the *locale* and scenes of the battle of Tetuan.

The war between Spain and Morocco cut out for him, as with a sabre stroke, his future career. He was then twenty-three years of age, thick-set, of powerful build, mercurial temperament, taciturn, resolute, and drilled to exertion. His tarrying in the East, which lasted from five to six months, was a revelation and a revel. He had never seen such light, such feasts of color, such figure compositions. It was here that he courted the sun and won him to the disclosure of his radiant mysteries. When the Emperor of Morocco arrived with his dashing suit to sign the treaty of peace, Fortuny was like a man driven to fever by the greatness of his opportunities. His hand flew over the pages of his note-book with lightning celerity.

What he was sent to Algiers to do he never really did, but he did other things of far greater import. While the commission of the Academy of Barcelona remained half finished, and was in that state on his studio wall when he died, he filled his mind with a series of magnificent themes, which in after years came to a perfect realization under his brush. Among these we find the stalls of the Moorish carpet sellers filled with the tumult of barter, the weary old Arabs sitting in the sun, and the pensive, sombre faces of snake charmers.

He addressed himself to etching and engraving, varying his eye with water colors of such virility as to rival works in oil. Fortuny's handicraft was something remarkable. He modeled splendid vases and decorated them with the shimmering tones of Hispano-Moresque; he wrought in metals, inlaying them with delicate designs of gold; he forged a famous sword with an ivory hilt, worthy of the battle-belt of a Moorish king. In the autumn of 1866 he went again to Paris and found friends in Rico, Ferrandez, and Zamacois. The last introduced him to M. Goupil, who at once gave recognition to his talent, and started for him a credit of 24,000 francs per year. He returned to Madrid to arrange for his nuptials with the daughter of M. Madrazo. May, 1868, brought him again to Rome. Here he steadily devoted himself to his great theme, "A Spanish Marriage." In this canvas and one other, "The Choice of a Model," Fortuny's gifts found their highest manifestation. Great men have sunbursts of expressional power, when talent is exalted into genius and when genius glows with the afflatus of an unearthly inspiration. Such was Delacroix's "Centaur Training the Young Achilles," Rousseau's "Le Givre," and Millet's "Sheepfold by Moonlight."

In 1870 Fortuny went to Granada to live, and installed himself at the Fonda de los Siete Suelos, on the same hill as the Alhambra, a short walk from the ancient palace of the Moorish kings. The quiet of the place, which had so charmed Henri Regnault, fascinated him. He counted the years spent there the sunniest of his life, writing to M. Simonetti :

"Figure to yourself the Villa Borghese on the summit of a mountain, surrounded by Moorish towns, and in the midst the most beautiful Arab palace, the elegance and ingenuity of ornament so great that the walls seem to be covered with guipure lace ! No suffering from heat, and one lives with such freedom that you might believe you were at home."

As indicative of the conscientious method through which Fortuny sought historical values for his easel, as well as the refreshment he perpetually brought to his eye, both in form and color, several letters are here opened.

To his comrade, M. Rico:

GRANADA, NOVEMBER 25, 1870.

DEAR MARTIN: I am delighted to learn that you feel inclined to come here. I think we can spend the winter profitably. We can paint courtyards and gypsies, when we please. Don't trouble yourself about Zamacois. He will not come, and if he did come he would not stay two weeks in Granada. You know his nature. This quiet and want of bustle would not suit him. I will trouble you to ask at the Escurial Library for an Asiatic manuscript of the year 1400, on the game of chess; it is illuminated with miniatures, certainly Italian; see if it contains costumes, arms, and other details suitable for paintings; in case it should I will have copies made for a small picture I intend to make.

Thine,

FORTUNY.

He was destined never again to meet Zamacois, who died suddenly from a seizure of angina pectoris.

GRANADA, MARCH, 1871.
Fonda de los Siete Suelos.

À MONSIEUR LE BARON DAVILLIER.

MY DEAR FRIEND: I am happy that nothing has happened to you in the midst of such misfortunes. I need not tell you how anxious I have been during the whole war in thinking of you; am hardly at ease now, for lo! the Commune again makes me tremble for you. As for me, I have some pictures begun, and many planned. Granada is an inexhaustible mine; but you know it and I will not dwell on it. I have a picture under way, and I hope it will turn out well, but it will be by making use of you for documents and details; no one at Paris can aid me better in this matter than you.

In regard to objects of art which I have met with, I will especially mention a very fine manuscript of the fifteenth century, ornamented with many well-preserved miniatures, and of the best style, with the arms and portrait of the owner, etc. I will have photographs of it made, and send them to you, that you may give me your opinion about it. I have some books on fencing, for Beaumont, and a curious note relating to arms copied from a paper of the fourteenth century.

Yours, FORTUNY.

After a long fight for daily bread, Fortuny surprised Fortune and swiftly turned into an Oriental prince, surrounded by masses of treasure, brilliant stuffs, Arabian war implements, glasses from Murano, vases from Pekin, malachite slabs resting on gilded satyrs, variegated marbles, and old tankards. There were four prime factors in the sum of Fortuny's life — Gavarni, the war in Morocco, Cecilia de Madrazo, and his blessed patron, Mr. William H. Stewart. Under these four captions one could write his entire history.

In the autumn of 1873 Fortuny changed his residence from the small house in the Via Gregoriana to a villa with surrounding gardens in the suburbs of the city. His studio adjoining offered space for the display of splendid fabrics, his *faïences* with sheens of gold, his ancient arms, and all his wealth of art objects, bronzes, and precious inlaid metals. A friend tells us "that he was petted and flattered by everybody."

Notwithstanding that, he was, as he said, "worried without knowing why." Was it a presentiment?

A projected visit to London occurred the first of June, and was prolific of inspirations. Here he met Millais, who welcomed him most cordially and exacted a promise of his return the following year. "I have so many souvenirs in my head, it will take me months to think it all out," he said. He left Paris for Rome, June 15th, accompanied to the Lyons station by his brother-in-law, Raymundo, and Baron Davillier, who embraced him, far from thinking that they should never see his face again. The fatal fever from which he suffered in 1869, returned with complications. He died November 21, 1874, at six o'clock in the evening, suffocated by vomiting blood. The personality of Fortuny has won a widening recognition, achieving a renown that must forever place him in front of the leading line of the artists of his century. Out of the large group of those who have done him honor, we choose a few voices to form a *symposium* upon his character and his art.

The Baron Davillier speaks: "Fortuny was above middle height, robust in appearance; the frankness and truthfulness of his character were reflected in his face, which was both handsome and sympathetic. He had a horror of etiquette and ceremony, and his natural timidity made him reserved, one might almost say a little rough, with those whom he knew not intimately, showing himself, on the contrary, very genial with those he loved, avoiding trivial talk and giving a serious turn to conversation. Surrounded by numerous flatterers, he distinguished, with extraordinary tact, true and disinterested friends from egotists, speculators, and false brothers in art. As for him, he was the truest and most devoted friend a man could find; he despised envy and never descended to a feeling so base.

"Fortuny had for music a very correct taste. Mozart and Beethoven were the masters he most admired. He loved reading much, especially the Latin historians and poets. His passion for curiosities is known. His collection, had he lived, would soon have become one of the most remarkable in Europe. His manual dexterity was marvelous, as the Moorish sword forged by him shows, of which the handle, inlaid with silver and carved in ivory, equals the most beautiful ancient work. I have not the knowledge necessary to judge of the talent of Fortuny. Every one knows that his individuality was very marked. If he had many imitators, it can be said he never sought to imitate any one."

We listen to M. Théophile Gautier in his official journal of May, 1870: "The name which has been oftenest spoken for the past four months in the world of art is surely that of Fortuny. One question never failed, when artists and amateurs met—'Have you seen Fortuny's paintings?' For Fortuny is a painter so marvelously original, of finished talent, sure of himself, although the artist was barely within the age of a competitor for the *Prix de Rome*. The traveled artists, and the students who came back from the Villa Medici, speak most highly of a young man admirably gifted, whom they consider of great force, working at Rome in a fantastic way, beyond all influence of schools. But the foreign name they mentioned, unsupported by any work, was not remembered. The 'Spanish Marriage,' the 'Serpent Charmer'—easel paintings; the 'Carpet Seller in Morocco,' the 'Café of the Swallows,' 'The Kief'—water colors, of a strength of tone that compete with oil, give an incontestable value to the name of Fortuny, and prove that the reports about him have not at all been exaggerated."

Prof. John C. Van Dyke, in an able review of this collection, prominently marks Fortuny: "There be artists who have harped on one note their life long, but Fortuny was not one of them. His was not a labored versatility, but a spontaneous and natural outburst. What others did by virtue of stubborn will, he apparently did with the strength and ease of genius. And how irresistible his few effective brush-strokes raise in us the sense and feeling of power! One night a dispute arose among some friends as to the position of a certain square in a Spanish city. Fortuny took a stick, wrapped around the end of it some frayed linen, mixed some ink and water together in a saucer, and upon some ordinary wrapping-paper drew the square, buildings, people, sky, air, and all; and to-day it hangs in Mr. Stewart's gallery as effective a 'black and white' as one would care to look upon."

M. Henri Regnault: "I have seen some of Fortuny's studies, which are prodigies of color and bold painting. Ah! what a painter that boy is! I have also seen two ravishing *eaux-fortes* by him. His pupil, Simonetti, who works in his studio, has shown me some charming things now under way. Two fine fellows, and how well they get on! What skill—how pleasing in color—what true genius—what spirit in the touch!

"Day before yesterday I passed the whole day with Fortuny, and that has broken my arms and legs—he is wonderful, that fellow! What marvels are in his house! He is master of us all. If you could see the two or three pictures he is now finishing, and the water colors he has recently completed!!! It is that which disgusts me with mine—oh, Fortuny! I can't sleep for you! I am not proud; Fortuny makes me pale with fear. I can no longer see what I have done or what I am doing. Look how a water color should be painted—what color, what charm, what drawing! Long live Spain—long live the East—long live Fortuny—immortality for Fortuny!"

M. Thomas Couture: "Oh, the beautiful things. I dreamed of them all night. They are the life, the light, the budding of spring, the colors with which God has painted the flowers. It is not painting, it is not work, it is not human. All sparkles with sunshine and genius; all is transformed by a magic prism. The vulgar becomes poetic, and satire amiable."

M. Charles Yriarte: "In his *genre* he was the head of a school. Endowed with a profound talent for manipulation, he created the *école de la main* (school of the hand). His science, united with a certain charm to which every one yielded; his love of light, his worship of the sun, and a unique something in the choice, the idea, and the rendering of his subjects, made for him a reputation which was legitimate. Fortuny has many imitators, but the majority of them fail to represent in their works, as he did, the character—the soul of things."

We pause for a moment ere we give audience to the voice of one who did more to shape the triumphant course of Fortuny than any other, whose cheer and strengthening sympathy passed like a sea breeze through the lungs of a tired man, whose tact and steadfast friendship braced the ambitions and gave fresh impulses to the ideals of this magician of art. We refer to Mr. William H. Stewart, of Philadelphia, the first American patron of Fortuny. We prelude his testimony with a letter which reveals his relations with the rising young men of his time. This letter was penned after Mr. Stewart himself had passed into the silence of the eternities. It is from M. Martin Rico to M. Montaignac, of Paris, the distinguished connoisseur:

DEAR FRIEND: It was about 1867 that I made the acquaintance of Mr. Stewart. He immediately ordered two landscapes of me, although I was then absolutely unknown. Since that time, whenever I returned from my travels, the first visit I received was from him and from my friend Madrazo, the two persons who took the deepest interest in me.

Although people may say that I am not disinterested in the matter, I take great pleasure in stating that I have never known a connoisseur more intelligent than Mr. Stewart and more untiring in seeking good pictures without ever considering the price. He had great influence at that time for the Spanish painters. The dealers hesitated in the selection of artists and the price to pay them, and it was he, with his delicate taste and correct eye, who discovered painters and interested himself in them.

He certainly was the greatest power at that moment in the artistic market of Paris.

I lost in Mr. Stewart a friend, a protector, and almost a father. He made his house ours, and I owe my position in great part to him. His greatest pleasure was the society of artists, and what I say for myself may be said also for Fortuny, Madrazo, Zamacoïs, and many others. He was the type of the most perfect *caballero* whom I have ever known, and you need only look at the collection of letters which the artists have written to him to be convinced of this. His gallery of pictures will show the world more than I can say.

Mr. Stewart, writing to Baron Davillier, says: "I heard of Mariano Fortuny for the first time in January, 1868, through Edward Zamacoïs, the much lamented and talented artist, who died at Madrid, January 12, 1871, at the early age of twenty-nine.

"He it was who took me to the Messrs. Goupil & Co., No. 9 Rue Chaptral, Paris, to see some ten very fine water colors, and pen-and-ink drawings, just received from Rome, with Fortuny's signature. Four of these were immediately secured by me at a very modest price, and two or three months later Zamacoïs brought me word from these dealers that they had an oil painting by Fortuny, and I must at once go with him to see it.

"We started on the instant, and found, at the Rue Chaptral, the 'Fantasia Arabe.' My companion went into ecstasies, calling it 'a pearl,' 'jewels,' etc., at the same time whispering to me to buy it, and not to let it slip at any price. The sum named was comparatively trifling, and this fine work became mine.

"I then determined to visit Rome and make the acquaintance of Fortuny, and in December, 1868, induced Zamacoïs, our common friend, to join me, telegraphing the artist in advance to engage rooms for us. I took with me a little painting by Meissonier, entitled 'Suite d'un Jeu des Cartes,' as Fortuny had requested his brother-in-law, Madrazo, I should do, having seen, up to that time, only photographs of this great master's works.

"On our arrival in the Eternal City we found him awaiting us at the railway depot, and were then conducted to the apartments he had engaged for us on the Corso, not far from his own residence. His reception of me was extremely cordial, frank, and open, for which, doubtless, I was indebted to Zamacoïs, of whom he was very fond. He soon took me into his intimate friendship, which terminated only with his death.

"In person, Fortuny was the *beau idéal* of an artist, in the full vigor of youth, with the build and strength of an athlete, and rather above the medium height. His head, perhaps, was a little too large, but highly intellectual, and covered with a profusion of dark-brown curly hair, and his eyes were a clear violet color, having a most anxious, inquiring expression. In manner he was quiet and serious, but of an affectionate, gentle, and most generous nature. Simply because I had complied with his modest request, in taking with me to Rome the little Meissonier painting mentioned above, he painted for me an aquarelle, called 'An Arab Street,' dedicated it to me as his friend, and it is now considered one of the finest gems in my collection. Henri Regnault served as a model for its principal and central figure. He obtained for me also another beautiful water color, which was nearly finished and on his easel, having been painted for d'Épinay, the French sculptor. This, and the 'Arab Street,' I carried back in my trunk to Paris, and would have been pleased to have taken everything he had.

"The 'Vicaria,' or 'Spanish Marriage,' was begun. I was not able to get it, as he was under contract to the Goupils, but he promised to finish the 'Academicians Choosing a Model,' which I gladly accepted in its stead, and have congratulated myself ever since on its acquisition.

"Some of the incidents of our stay in Rome will tend to prove the admiration in which he was held by those eminent artists, Zamacoïs and Regnault. The latter asked him why he never exhibited in the Paris Annual Salon, and he replied: 'I have never anything worth the showing, and I am not a Frenchman; but why don't you?' 'I have nothing,' answered Regnault. 'Then,' said Fortuny, 'go and ask d'Épinay for the head you gave him; it is excellent. You can add some canvas, and make a capital picture.'

"Regnault took his advice, got the head and carried it to Spain, and the result was the now celebrated painting, known as 'Salome,' which he exhibited the following year, with his portrait of General Prim.

"One day, while we were in his studio watching him at work, he asked Zamacoïs to paint something for him as a souvenir of his visit. Zamacoïs began at once on a small panel the figure of 'Arlequino,' Fortuny's favorite man model, and after working three or four hours and scratching out as many times, he gave up in despair, threw the little board into a corner, and said to me: 'Don Guillermo, *no puedo mas!*' (I cannot do any more.) We went into the garden, and Zamacoïs exclaimed: 'I can now breathe freely, but I cannot do so where Mariano paints! He absorbs all the light, color, and air; in fact, he is enough to disgust one with one's own work, for he is the only one who can paint!'

"On this same garden opened the studios of Moragas and the Duchess Casteglioné Colonna. The latter, known in art circles as Marcello, the sculptress, professed the greatest admiration for Fortuny and profited largely by her proximity to his studio and the advice given therein. This may be seen in her bronze statue of a 'Fury,' under the main stairway of the Paris Opera House.

"As stated by Davillier, in the spring of 1870 Fortuny came to the French capital, and installed himself and family in the Maison Valin, on the Champs Elysées. Here he finished the 'Vicaria,' and his three most important aquarelles, 'The Reader,' 'The Turkish Carpet Dealer,' and the 'Torrero.' While at work on the 'Vicaria,' the artist Meissonier dropped in to see him, just as he was in need of a suitable model for a cavalry officer, whom he wished to introduce into the picture. Hearing of his want, the great French artist said: 'I am the only man who has the proper legs for the character you need, and if you will come out to Poissy I will serve as your model.'

"Fortuny accepted, went to Poissy, and painted to the life this wonderful man. I am the happy possessor of this remarkable and curious portrait of Meissonier by Fortuny, through the generosity of his widow, who presented it to me after her husband's death. The fact that Meissonier served as a model to the younger painter reveals the former's admiration, and that he was seriously impressed by this great genius, cannot be doubted.

"A strange and sudden death occurred at the Maison Valin while Fortuny was staying there. Canaveral, a friend of his, came from Spain with about one hundred old paintings and some drawings, and went to the same house. Fortuny, assisted by Zamacoïs and Rico, endeavored to clean and arrange these paintings for exhibition, so that they might be sold for the benefit of his friend, but for a fortnight no purchaser appeared. At last a well-known dealer called, and fell dead while looking at the collection, and poor Canaveral failed to effect any sales. If I had not bought from him a very beautiful aquarelle, painted by our artist, and doubtless a present to his old friend, Canaveral would have been without the means to return home with his pictures.

"At that time I was residing in the Avenue d'Jena, and I shall never forget the day of Victor Noir's burial. He had been killed a few days before by Prince Pierre Bonaparte, at Auteuil. It seemed as if the entire working population of Paris had turned out, dressed in clean blouses, and armed with implements of their different trades, to do honor to the dead, or mischief to the living who might oppose their demonstration. I started from home about ten in the morning, to go, with Zamacoïs and Fortuny, on a visit to Meissonier, at Poissy. We met this crowd of ill-disposed operatives marching toward Neuilly, the residence of the mother of the deceased. Returning to Paris at 4.30 P.M., we parted with Zamacoïs at the St. Lazare station, and Fortuny and I, taking a cab together, started for our homes, but on attempting to cross the Champs Elysées, near the Palais d'Industrie, we were prevented by a large body of cavalry and artillery which occupied the space from the Rond Point to the Place de la Concorde.

"Facing this military mass was another, of nearly 100,000 blouses, filling the Avenue des Champs Elysées as far as the Arc de Triomphe, and far beyond, into the Avenue de la Grande Armée. Arm in arm they came marching towards the troops, singing the Marseillaise, and headed by Henri Rochefort, who was riding in a cab. It appears that he had fainted once or twice during the day, from excitement or from fear of failure in his undertaking, which was to conduct the crowd past the Tuileries Palace.

"We were, of course, obliged to make a great detour, in order to reach our homes. This was the beginning of the end of the Second Empire, which was overthrown on the 4th of September following.

"About this time my wife, being anxious to have a portrait of me by Fortuny, asked him to paint one. He immediately said he would if she would let him have his painting of the 'Antiquary.' Taking this with him, he obtained a photograph of me, and a few days later returned the painting with my portrait introduced, which is considered by artists and friends to be a most striking likeness. This same picture of the 'Antiquary' he had given, a year or two previous, to Capo Bianchi, the dealer in Rome, in exchange for an Arab gun and a broken Venetian glass, these articles being worth about 200 francs.

"Madrazo and I have often remarked that what seemed to strike strangers, on entering Fortuny's studio, was himself, more than his work. The living picture was really interesting : one could not fail to be impressed by that fine intellectual head, with its regular but expressive features; his appearance of full, vigorous health, and his becoming, careless dress. His wife, in the bloom of her youth and beauty, seated by his side and mending an old piece of tapestry while he painted, lent a charm to the picture, well calculated to draw one's first glances from even his brilliant creations.

"Many of his evenings were passed at our house. He was fond of music and conversation, to both of which he was an attentive listener, though preferring often to be drawing, in which he frequently indulged when with us. He would sometimes take away with him a photographic portrait of some head or person which happened to strike his fancy, and copy it most exactly in India ink or sepia. In this way I have the likeness of one Amos Foster, known at Torresdale, Philadelphia, as 'Bos'—copied so closely by Fortuny that it is difficult to distinguish it from the photograph.

"It was about this time that the 'Vicaria' was finished and upon its easel. One day a gentleman called and, after admiring the picture greatly, said he would like to own something by the same artist. Messrs. Goyena and Madrazo being present, acted as interpreters, as Fortuny could not then speak French, and replied that he could not promise, as he was under contract to the Goupils. The visitor, expressing much regret at this, concluded by giving Fortuny *carte blanche* to paint whatever he pleased for him without regard to price, handed his card to Goyena, and departed. Goyena read aloud his card :

" ' MONSIEUR DUGLAIRY,

" ' *Chef du Café Anglais.*'

"Fortuny received it as a pleasantry, and would not believe the fact until he had read the card himself. The three friends, however, determined to visit this culinary artist and breakfast at his celebrated café the following day. When the hour arrived they entered the dining-rooms and said they preferred giving their orders to the *chef*, who shortly appeared. Recognizing the trio, he made many apologies for the manner in which his art suffered, owing to the use of mineral coal in the economic cooking-ranges now in use, but said he would do his best. He gave them indeed a splendid repast, after which he invited them to visit his Japanese collection, valued by experts at more than one million francs. And this man is the head cook, and one of the present proprietors of the Café Anglais !

"Fortuny left Paris late in the spring for Spain, and established himself and family in the Alhambra at Granada, in company with Rico and Ricardo Madrazo. Here he started work on some of his finest inspirations. Little dreaming that we should be separated from Fortuny for so long a time by the Franco-Prussian War, we started for Trouville, where we spent the months of July, August, September, and part of October. The Prussian lines, however, were extending in every direction and encompassing the French, so I deemed it prudent to take my family to

Torquay, England, where we passed nearly six months agreeably, occasionally hearing from Fortuny and Rico through Zamacoïs and Don Federico Madrazo, both of whom resided in Madrid.

"On the 12th of January, 1871, Zamacoïs died in Madrid, and the sad news was announced to us by a letter from his widow, dated three days later.

"Immediately after the surrender of Paris I went over with Saintin, a French artist, to the conquered capital for the purpose of looking after my affairs, and three or four days after our arrival the reign of the Commune began. We remained, however, three weeks or more, until it became too hot for us, and then persuaded Madrazo—who had passed through the siege, serving manfully in the American Ambulance—to return to England with us, and in April we all moved to London. A week later Goupil & Co., who were established in the English metropolis, sent me word that they had received from Granada three paintings by Fortuny and two by Rico. We went to see them, and I bought two of Fortuny's and one of Rico's paintings.

"When the Commune was put down we returned to France, entering Paris two days after the Versailles or government troops took possession, and were in time to witness the Tuileries, the Hôtel de Ville, the Treasury, the Palace of the Legion of Honor, and other buildings, still burning, and smouldering in ruins.

"In the fall of 1871, during my absence in the United States, Fortuny sent two oil paintings to the Goupils. They were bought by MacLean, of London, who, failing to dispose of them without loss in England, returned them to Goupil for sale, where I found them on my return, and at once purchased both. It was evident that the British public did not appreciate Fortuny, nor had the French learned full confidence in his genius, till after his third visit to Paris, in 1873. As I was again absent in America at this time, I had not the pleasure of seeing him until the spring of 1874.

"During his stay at the Alhambra he worked hard, and in the numerous letters I received from him while there, he expressed the greatest enjoyment in his occupations, and in the beauty, the quiet, and the climate of Granada. At times he sent me photographs, and, again, pen-and-ink drawings of what he had done or was doing. In this way I was able to order the paintings owned by the Honorable Mr. A. E. Borie, and Mr. H. W. Gibson, of Philadelphia. Before leaving Granada for Rome, he sent a beautiful little oil painting of a fruit-stall, painted at the Alhambra, in which he introduced his wife and children, as a souvenir to Mrs. Stewart.

"From Rome he continued his intimate correspondence with me, all his letters containing beautiful sketches and drawings, which I have preserved most carefully as marvels of art.

"In 1874, as stated above, he came again to Paris, bringing with him the 'Academicians Choosing a Model,' which he painted for me; the 'Poet's Garden,' bought by Mr. Heeren; 'An Arab Horseman,' and a 'Torso,' for Mr. Errazu; 'A

Large Arab,' with a wonderful background of carpets ; ' A Lady in a Garden' ; · The Cochinos,' a study of flowers, and the 'Roman Carnival.' The last three he took back to Italy, intending to keep them for himself. During this last visit I saw a great deal of him, and he left us, to return to Rome, in good spirits, saying that he was going to paint to please himself and not the dealers. He complained, however, of his digestion, and was obliged to be very careful in his diet, but none of his friends gave the slightest thought to his complaint.

"On Sunday, the 22d of November, 1874, Madrazo, Rico, and Saintin came to breakfast with me. After we had finished, Madrazo told us he had received a telegram the night previous, announcing Fortuny's illness, and asking him to proceed to Rome immediately, but as the dispatch came too late he was unable to take the express train until that same Sunday evening. We all concluded Fortuny's case was desperate, and could only hope for the best.

"They left me, but at six in the evening Rico returned, sobbing, scarcely able to utter the words, 'He is dead.'

"The truth is, he died before the first dispatch was sent, as the second proved, which was sent simply to hasten Madrazo's departure. This was the end of one of the best of men and one of the greatest artists of his time."

GAVARNI

WE are in the presence of the greatest character draughtsman France has ever known. His family name, Guillaume Sulpice Chevalier, is lost under his famous *nom de plume*. Born in Paris, 1804; died, 1866. Chevalier of the Legion of Honor. He played with his pencil in childhood, but had attained his majority when he met M. Blaisot, who gave him an order for an album of sketches. In 1824 he went to Bordeaux to execute works for the engraver Adam, but soon broke with him, and set out for the Pyrenees on a walking tour. At Tarbes he made the acquaintance of M. Leden, the Registrar of the Signal Service, who bore him company on many of his excursions. He filled his book with peasants in all phases of their life and costumes. He returned to Paris in May, 1828, still busy with types, sketching constantly, but failing to earn money. It was suggested that he should interview Susse, the dealer, and exhibit his water colors. Susse was willing to purchase his collection on the condition that he should sign them. Seizing a pen, he wrote "Gavarni," and from that moment lost his baptismal name. Gradually he gravitated to his real vocation: caricature, the art of the grotesque for purposes of satire.

This is preëminently the art of the modern ages. There was small hint of it among the ancients, only three *papyri* of a satirical tendency being known to exist in Egyptian archives, and these are more droll than ironical. The Greeks had gifts for pictorial parody, as shown in antique vases sketched with burlesque themes; the Romans put the grotesque into plastic expression, as seen in frescoes unearthed at Pompeii and Herculaneum; but the caricaturists of the olden time must be sought for rather in the poets and dramatists than among painters and sculptors. Through the long dusk of the middle ages any quantity of material was amassed for the study of the grotesque, but it was unvitalized, without form, and voiceless.

The art of pictorial irony was born in the birth-pangs of the Renaissance. It is said that the earliest genuine example (1499) is a comic gravure relating to Louis XII. and his Italian war. The Reformation in Germany led to a full seeding for satirical ephemeræ. The prototypes of the cartoons that smirk from the pages of *Punch* and *Charivari* are the heads of Martin Luther and Alexander VI. In England the sixteenth century was innocent of this charge, the only exception being a feeble effort to show Mary Stuart as a mermaid. The eighteenth century was preëminently the age of caricature, evidenced in the domain of literature as in that of art. Smith, Smollett, and Fielding, no less than Hogarth and Gillray, were expert in ironics. In the hands of Gillray political caricature became almost epic in majesty of conception, breadth of treatment, and far-reaching suggestiveness. An English critic remarks "that it is to the works of this man of genius that historians must turn for the popular reflection of all the political *notabilia* of the end of the eighteenth and the beginning of the nineteenth century." Spain discovers an artist capable of competing with the English group in the works of Francis Goya, which are described by Théophile Gautier as a mixture of Rembrandt, Watteau, and the comical dreams of Rabelais. Champfleury discerns analogies between him and Honoré Daumier, the greatest caricaturist of modern France.

Daumier was ideal in carrying a single character through a series of pictures, showing with each some fresh travesty; such were Robert Macaire, Bertrand, and Ratapoil. In one he shows the country politician canvassing for votes, seeking, as usual, to save the people. Mr. Henry James thus uncovers this admirable page: "A sordid but astute peasant, twirling his thumbs on his stomach and looking askance, allows the political adviser to urge upon him in a whisper that there is not a minute to lose—to lose for action, of course—if he wishes to keep his wife, his house, his field his heifer, and his calf. The canny skepticism in the ugly, half-averted face of the typical rustic, who considerably suspects his counselor, is indicated by a few masterly strokes. This is what the student of Daumier recognizes as his science, or, if the word has a better grace, his art. It is what has kept life in his work so long after so many of the occasions of it have been swept into darkness."

Journalism and caricature were often workers in the same field up to 1845, but the alliance was uncertain and brief. It became the mission of Charles Philipon, the peculiar and emphatic exploiter of comic journalism, to make it lasting. *La Caricature*, founded by Philipon in 1831, and suppressed in 1833, was followed by *La Charivari*. It is here that we find Gavarni, who brought modern social caricature, in its present guise, to a perfect expressional form.

The Commune was a forcing process for the production of artists of this school who were well endowed with both ability and bitterness. Gavarni ranks foremost among these pictorial satirists. The years between 1840 and 1847 may be taken as his best period. As a recorder of the manners of his time, he produced work possessing the purest qualities, with such seriousness of aim as to insure it permanent place and consideration. He was the mate of Balzac; his peer in power and his intimate friend. Any effort to pass in review Gavarni's artistic record would be wearisome. The following are a few of his examples that have found enthusiastic appreciation: "The Impostures of Women in Some Matters of Sentiment," "Dreams," "The Muses," "Lessons and Counsels," "The Martyrs," "The Students of Paris," "The Terrible Children," "Masks and Visages."

JEAN LÉON GÉRÔME

EVERY official honor that can fall at the feet of a great artist in France has fallen to Léon Gérôme. He has been a Commander of the Legion since 1878, a member of the Institute since 1875, a professor of the École des Beaux Arts since 1863.

The Medal of Honor has been given to him twice. His creations are distributed throughout the museums, public galleries, and great private collections of the world. He has a cabinet filled with decorations in bronze and gold. Gérôme was born in the Haute-Saône, at Vesoul, on the 11th day of May, 1824.

He won his first medal in the Salon of 1847 by "The Fighting Cocks." While he was executing this picture he said to Delaroche: "I try to paint honestly, clinging to nature, but I am still unskillful; it is flat and thin." "Yes," his master responded, "you are right, but there are originality and style. You will do better later; in the meantime do not be anxious; exhibit your picture—exhibit it. It will do you honor." His picture was "skied." Nevertheless the near-sighted Gautier managed to discover the "Cock Fight," and the day following wrote in the columns of *La Presse:* "Let us mark with white this lucky year, for unto us a painter is born. He is called Gérôme. I tell you his name to-day, and to-morrow it will be celebrated."

He was the pupil of Delaroche, whom he followed to Rome half a century ago. He visited Russia and Egypt, finding in the latter a wealth of suggestion for his brush. It was not in the studies of his first visit to Egypt that he disclosed his real power. These are superficially captivating and of easy translation through the average conventional keys found in Orientalism. Edmond About was not astray concerning this period of Gérôme's work when he said: "His views in Egypt are interesting, apart from the merit of execution, which is little. One finds in them neither a very profound study of form, nor a very active feeling of strength, nor a very passionate love of color." The public differed from About's judgment, and crowded to see these productions. It was at this time that Gérôme hung his "Duel After a Masked Ball." Few pictures have become so familiar to the popular eye. The artist has coldly taken his theme and rendered it with fearful force. He reveals the weight of the invisible tiger of remorse already bending the shoulders of the victor as he goes away into the ghastly dawn. The central figure of the lifeless Pierrot, the victim of that encounter, is beyond criticism. The man has not swooned; he is not dying—he is *dead*. The "Death of Cæsar" might be placed as a pendant to the "Duel." It has been said that in Gérôme's initial draft for this canvas the body of Cæsar, lying prostrate before the statue of Pompey, was the only figure in the deserted hall, while bloody footprints, intermingled and confused, leading toward the door, alone told of the flight of the murderers. Should this gossip be true the artist marred his tragic story by massing gesticulating, fleeing senators in the background, and spoiled the stern simplicity of his original conception. Art may be greater in what it suggests than in what it plainly tells.

Gérôme exhibited in 1855 "Le Siècle d'Auguste." He seeks to embrace in one vast canvas the reign of Augustus, which was the culmination of pagan history. From this apex, civilization slowly declines into the deepening shadows of the middle ages. Alfred Tanouarn, in 1860, thus paragraphs the picture: "Augustus is on his throne, overlooking the scene. Near him is stationed a young man virile in form, a symbolic image of the genius of Rome. At the right of the prince are the political notabilities of the epoch, on his left the artists and poets. Farther away, upon the lower steps of the temple, lies the body of the assassinated Cæsar, before which Cassius and Brutus are standing erect, the former holding a dagger; opposite, the dead bodies of Cleopatra and Antony are thrown upon each other; below, on both sides, the conquered people seem to be adoring the majesty of triumphant Rome. Finally are seen the infant Jesus, Mary, and Joseph—a mystic group that an angel covers with its wings. This is an intermediate work between history and allegory." It is manifest that the artist's purpose was to show the power by which revolutions were to turn the world through the gates of new horizons; the power was the

Christ-child shielded by wings. This painting gained for Gérôme the red ribbon. Soon after he started again for Egypt.

Writing to a friend, he says : "Probably among my ancestors a Bohemian must have slipped in, for I have a nomadic tendency and the bump of locomotion." He saw Egypt with fresh eyes and matured mind. When we study the output of this second journey into the Nile valley, we are conscious of coming face to face with history, tabulated with rare precision and strength. At the close of the Salon of 1874 he obtained the Grand Medal and touched a prime which has since simply refused to wane. In the Universal Exhibition at Paris in 1878, Gérôme uncovered his hand as a sculptor. His "Combat of the Gladiators" obtained wide recognition and emphatic praise. It is said that when he has "failed to find any detail of armor or costume that was necessary to finish his work he would leave the Boulevard de Clichy for the Naples Museum, make sketches there of what he desired, and returning to his atelier by the express train, continue his labor and reinstall himself before his group in clay, that had not hardened during this rapid journey to Italy."

Fifteen years ago it was the privilege of the writer to meet him in his splendid studio. The picture known as "The Two Majesties" was on an easel. A lion with lifted front, from a projecting rock, across leagues of landscape, calmly faced the rising sun. It was impossible to restrain the inward whisper: "Here are not two, but three majesties—the lion, the sun, and Gérôme; the last having on his brow the flash of a triple crown."

EDWARD JOHN GREGORY

THIS artist recalls the note struck by Alfred Parsons in English landscape work. He has produced portraits of quiet charm and attained significant regard from connoisseurs. He was born in Southampton, 1850. First studied in the Southampton and then at the South Kensington art schools, subsequently in the École des Beaux Arts. Carolus Duran was his master. He is a member of the Institute of Painters in Water Color, and was made an A. R. A. in 1883. He is represented here by an interesting example in black and white, "The War in the East."

HENRI HARPIGNIES

WE confront a passionate lover of art in Henri Harpignies. His birthplace was Valenciennes; his advent July 28, 1819. Equally in oil and water colors he has taken highest rank. He studied with Achard, visited Italy, and made his manners to the Salon in 1853, since which date he has exhibited regularly. His "Evening in the Roman Campagna" received a medal in 1866, which was so cordially granted that it repaired somewhat the neglect of the year preceding. This picture is at the Luxembourg. He was medaled in 1868 and 1869; second class, 1878; Legion of Honor, 1875; Officer, 1883. Harpignies came of a wealthy family of merchants, who restrained his tendency to art. He was twenty-seven years old when he appeared in the studio of Achard, who was the dignified embodiment of academic methods. Upon a certain occasion, after searching far for picturesque views, both found themselves in the magnificent valley of Crémieux. Achard told his pupil that he did not care to have him undertake a number of studies; that two would be sufficient—an effect of growing day and another of evening lights. Harpignies began, and had one well advanced. The interpretation was of remarkable sincerity, but a slight limitation awaited his gifts. In a corner of the landscape was a group of small trees, the rare foliage of which seemed like frosted lace blown about by the wind. The hand of Harpignies lacked the lightness required for the rendering of such a delicate subject. For eight days he struggled, rubbed out, began again and again, only to efface his efforts. On the ninth day he said to himself that the trees did not stand for any important value in his landscape, so he quietly suppressed them behind a tint of azure. After this deed he returned, satisfied at having given a lesson to Nature. But he had calculated without his master. When Achard came to inspect his work, there was a glance of surprise, then of incredulity, then of greater surprise; finally a frown of indignation, followed by an explosion, as, with angered voice, he thundered: "Sir, you will have those trees in your picture to-morrow, or you will go home." There came a time when Harpignies was not less exacting with himself, which accounts for his enduring hold on fame. He was a scientific student of values in color, proceeding at the first with "neutrals." He is unsurpassed in his balancing of sky and water, in composing, and then translating the harmony of masses. He was devoted to music. Here is a line from his note-book: "One must play with the brush as one plays with the strings of a violin."

This reveals the order of his art; there was no wayward impulse defying the regnant tones of nature. He sought only to enter the sweep of her rhythmic laws, striking the chords as light strikes a cloud, "drawing color for a tune, with a vibrant touch."

In the foreground of our time, his figure, tall, robust, square-shouldered, groups naturally, though much younger, with Diaz, Rousseau, and Dupré. His productions affirm that landscape art was not buried when Corot died.

FERDINAND HEILBUTH

THIS artist was at first merely a colorist of costumes. It was at Rome he unveiled his unique talent for treating the life and manners of the pontifical court. This was done with such intelligent discrimination, subtle humor, and keen insight that Heilbuth entered at once upon a field of broadening renown. He was born in Hamburg in 1826, but naturalized in France. He took his medals under the second class in 1857-1859 and 1861; Legion of Honor, 1861; Officer of the same, 1881. He died in Paris in 1889. His "Le Mont de Piété" is at the Luxembourg. He exhibited at the Royal Academy, London, in 1871, two pictures—"Spring" and "On the Banks of the Seine"; also at Berlin, same year, "The Autumn of Love." He was surnamed "the painter of cardinals," so loyally did he render these cheery old gentlemen in red. Between the years 1852 and 1862 he oscillated between *genre* and historical themes, successfully sending to exhibitions those works which brought him marked successes: "Rubens Presents Brauwer to his Wife," "The Son of Titian," "Tasso at the Court of Ferrara," "A Concert at a Cardinal's Home," "The Pawn Shop," "The Promenade," and "The Cardinal's Antechamber." Heilbuth forgetting his master, M. Comte, and surrendering himself without reserve to the world of impressions at Rome, has certainly created a style of his own. To those who were strangers to Heilbuth in 1855, it will be a surprise to learn that the artist of to-day, so robust and resonant, was at that period "a pale, thin dreamer under the falling autumn leaves." He needed the sun of the south in his blood, and returning to Rome, caught for his inspiration the typical forms, brilliant contrasts, and picturesque tones of the Vatican, becoming its recognized painter. His "Monte Pincio," with the clergy in their glowing robes and official dignities on the one side and the royal procession of the House of Savoy on the other, has not only great artistic value, but for those who, in the future, will seek to reconstruct the Rome of the pontiffs, before united Italy seized the city for its capital, it has the intrinsic weight of an historical document.

In 1870 Heilbuth initiated a departure which may be said to have constituted for him a new style, if not his last incarnation. His life in England, where he spent two years, profoundly touched and swayed his spirit. He was open to fresh views, was accessible to the latest revelation. The beauty of English landscapes and of English women, the open air of their social high life, were the forces that now differentiated his career. The aristocracy were in turn captivated, and acclaimed him their fashion and fad. He painted a famous picture, "Repose after a Cricket Game," owned by Sir Richard Wallace. In 1872 he returned to Paris, and, notwithstanding his wanderings, his tarrying in Rome, his English episode, came to be ranked as the artist of the *Grand Monde Parisien*. As a water-colorist he dates from 1864, and has poured out a mass of gems, full of grace and poetry. He was fond of the greensward, the entrance squares of *châteaus*, placing in his landscapes girls in fashionable summer toilets. He specially affected them in white or pearl-grey dresses, accented with black belt and long black gloves. About these he would fling the bloom of his atmospheres, finely toned with the virginal beauty of the costumes and the verdure of the fields. He has been termed "the Watteau of the century." His study of "A Lady in Yellow" commands unstinted admiration. Heilbuth was prominent in founding the Society of French Aquarellists.

DON GERMAN HERNANDEZ

A PUPIL of the San Fernando Academy, this Spanish artist has justified the prophecies of his kindred, and promises to rank high in the record of his future work.

Although Mr. Stewart secured only "The Head of a Woman" from his easel, he bought with it a type of the best art executed in the Spain of to-day. Every canon is conserved and made luminous—form, color, poise, and that other equation without which the body is but featured clay—the divine glow and pulse of life itself. This lovely face is a prelude to creations that must follow after, as day follows dawn.

THEODOR HORSCHELT

A MARTIAL soul was encased in the body of Horschelt. For him art must lead to the camp life of the soldier and the tumult of battle. He was originally taught in the Munich Academy, and later by Hermann Auschutz, a famous martinet and drill-master in drawing. His first picture was of such virility as to find a purchaser in the Society of Arts at Munich—"The Wild Huntsman." He studied horses in the royal stables at Stuttgart, and was a favorite with the reigning house. When he had barely passed his majority he visited Spain and Algiers; in 1858 shared in the Russian expedition to the Caucasus, accompanying Alexander II. and Albert of Prussia in their inspection of the armies, returning to his home city, after five years of absence, by way of Moscow and St. Petersburg. This period of his career was filled with incessant labor, producing many pictures in oils and water colors. The siege of Strasbourg found him busy with sketch-book in the midst of stirring scenes. From the sources indicated, Horschelt put forth most effective canvases, having the zest of adventure and battle. His series of illustrations of "Chamois Hunting in the Bavarian Mountains" has been engraved.

In 1854, by royal request, he painted for the King of Würtemberg "The Rest of Arabs in the Desert." His "Arabian Horse" and "A Moorish Camp at Algiers" immediately followed. His later works reveal the march of untiring talent. The "Storming of the Entrenchments of Schamyl on Mount Gunib" took the first medal at the exposition of 1867, through which he was made Chevalier of the Order of the Iron Crown of Austria. The Russian Emperor decorated him with the Orders of Stanislaus and Saint Anna. His "Morning in the Bedouin Camp" and "A Cavalry Attack" are two water colors that have attracted attention. He was fond of freeing his humor in small pen-and-ink sketches, caricaturing in the mood of the famous "Cham" of Paris. Horschelt had the deep pleasure of finding in his art an outlet and unfolding of personal tastes and aspirations to the fullest limit of forceful, fiery utterance.

LUDWIG KNAUS

ACCEPTED by Germany as her greatest painter of *genre* and by the world as one of the chief representatives of that art, Professor Knaus has behind him a trail of honors. He was born at Wiesbaden in 1829; his father was an optician. He studied under Jacobi, and at the age of fifteen entered the Düsseldorf Academy, then dominated by Sohn and Schadow. He yielded chiefly to two influences in the formative period of his art: the old Dutch masters and the noblest leaders of the modern French school. He was never, in any pulse beat of his existence, a Düsseldorfian. Member of the Academies of Berlin, Vienna, Munich, Amsterdam, Antwerp, and Christiania; Officer of the Legion of Honor; Knight of the Order of Merit. Medaled at Paris, Berlin, Weimar, he has justified in his career every distinguished recognition.

At the age of twenty he had nothing to learn in the mere manipulation of the brush; it only remained for him to perfect himself on lines of larger value. His has been a steady growth, each output from his hand revealing finer and riper fruit. His ambition did not take him above the common people in his choice of subjects. These he sought to know in an intimate, familiar fellowship and to portray their customs, joys, griefs, their life battle, whose only armor was very plain daily raiment, but whose breasts were shields behind which the conflicts of humanity were fought out. Knaus renounced idealistic, mythological compositions of his German brethren for the realities of this world. Wherever life was in its normal mould, untravestied, free of masks, without pomposities and parade, there was his atelier. He has decided fondness for the peasant in all his phases, his simplicity with its cunning, his *naïve* self-regard when honored. All his works are significant utterances for the reason that they are so perfectly composed and, from the standpoint of the eye, exactly express the subject. He treats the events of current life with such wit, charm, pathos, loyalty, that everyone is delighted, understands, and will not forget. Edmond About, in 1855, writes: "I do not know whether Herr Knaus has long nails, but even if they were as long as those of Mephistopheles it should still be said that he was an artist to his finger-ends. His pictures please the Sunday public, the Friday public, the critics, the *bourgeoisie*, and, it may be said, the painters too. The connoisseur is won by his knowledge and thorough ability; the most incompetent are attracted by his canvases because they tell pleasant anecdotes. Herr Knaus has capacity for satisfying every one. He has met his mission and filled it, winning a firm, sure place in the affections of the people and the highest coronation in art."

LOUIS EUGÈNE LAMI

A FRIEND of David, Géricault, Gérard, Girodet, and Prudhon needs no formal presentation. The man of such comradeship must have the artist full grown in his heart. Eugène Lami was equipped with every quality that enters into the personal adjustment of a strong painter to his sphere. He began at the beginning, and patiently drilled under the instruction of Corot, Horace Vernet, and the École des Beaux Arts. He reached the Legion of Honor in 1837; was made Officer, 1862; medaled in 1865. His first laurels were won as a water colorist of scenes in fashionable life. Historical representation had a firm fascination for him, and eventually took large grasp on his mind. When released as tutor to the Orleans princes, he gave himself to travel, visiting Italy, England, Belgium, everywhere alert for the realization of his ideals. In this wandering term he painted "Charles I. Receiving a Rose on his Way to Prison," "A Combat in the Campaign of the Balkans," "A Rustic Team," "Course and Clocher, Muscovite Bravery." These were followed by more imposing examples, in which he exploits his passion for historic pieces. We have the "Combat of Wattignies," "Capitulation d'Anvers," "The Battle of Alma," "The Combat of Hondschoote" (Museum of Lille).

In all of the foregoing the landscape parts were painted by Jules Dupré. After the fall of Louis Philippe in 1848, Lami left France for England. He was accompanied by the satirist Gavarni, whose influence over him may be traced in several of his later productions. Lami gave himself entirely to water color during his English residence, entering upon a series of works to illustrate the most luminous scenes in Shakespeare, Byron, and Goethe. This literary endeavor was a bold attempt to think the thoughts of these men of genius into forms and colors. He wedded his art to expressions which, in many instances, were incomparably finer than the original texts he illustrated.

A marvelous water color, based on Shakespeare's suggestion, reveals Cleopatra, who, vanquished, receives the visit of Cæsar. The artist has clearly shown in Cæsar the Roman who spoke to the conquered Queen in these words: "Stand up! Do not kneel down; I beg you stand up! Stand up, *Egypt!*" Lami was often great in his composition, as instanced in the Huguenots showing the "Blessing of the Poignards," and, again, in the picture of young "Marie Stuart Forced to Listen to the Preaching of John Knox."

Another masterpiece is a scene from Sir Walter Scott's "Ivanhoe." In characterizing an epoch of his own time, he fearlessly lashes the flanks of the nobility.

"A Double Team of the Prince Demidoff" underscores the high life of 1836. His finesse in satire is here shown, and we understand why Gavarni found in Lami a friend. This portraiture of Demidoff, a lion of the kingdom of Louis Philippe, is a match for Zamacois's canvas, the "Education of a Prince." There is much to be said upon the scope and variety of Lami's palette. To signalize a brief list gives a glance into his fecund brain : "Bal de Tuileries," "Course à Chantilly," "Revue de Chasseurs," "The Orgie," "The Marble Stairs of Versailles," "The Navy of Cherbourg," "The Baptism of Louis XIII." He gave twelve studies to the chronicles of Charles IX., illumined the writings of De Musset, and illustrated with brilliant designs the Faust of Gounod. These were phrased with melodic motives, and uttered chastened passions through symphonies of color.

WILHELM LEIBL

A SON of the conductor of music in the cathedral at Cologne, Leibl came to his inheritance under helpful influences. He was born October 23, 1844. In his first years of manhood he strikingly resembled Courbet, both in physique and *genre* gravitations, having like faculty of eye and hand, while in traits of personal character he radically contrasted the flaming Frenchman, being reticent, self-contained, and exclusive in his choice of friends. His organization foreordained him to art. He is at his highest point of expression when treating the lowliest themes ; the simple-hearted maiden radiant in the freshness of rustic life, the old grandmother whose sweet face is webbed with wrinkles, and the peasant who strikes the earth daily to find his bread. There is a cynical clique who affect to find great art only in imposing subjects that bulk largely on the historic page or fly abroad in the spectacular involutions of classic composition, whereas there is no such thing as great or little art, judging by such a standard. Art takes its significance from the treatment which a subject receives at the hands of the artist. There are great subjects, small subjects, but the art lies in the interior grasp and subtle skill of the painter.

No man, after Professor Knaus, more explicitly illustrates this than Leibl. His masterpiece is in the collection before us; the subject, "Village Politicians." These types balance him in a sphere with François Millet, in the fashion in which Holbein correlated Michel Angelo.

A letter from the artist to Mr. W. H. Stewart fittingly falls into space here:

AISLING IN OBERBAYERN.

MY DEAR MR. STEWART: Permit me to earnestly request that you will lend me the picture, painted by me, entitled "Peasants" ("Village Politicians"), now in your possession, that I may exhibit it in this year's great International Exhibition, which will be held in Berlin. For some years past various directors of art exhibitions have urged me to make some arrangement by which this picture, which is very little known in Germany, might be placed before the art-loving public. Because I felt, however, that this would perhaps occasion you some trouble, I have not ventured, in spite of earnest appeals, to approach you upon the subject. But now, at the request of the Berlin Academy of Fine Arts (of which, for some years, I have been a member), that I should exhibit my best picture in this year's great international art show, I write to you for permission to use the "Peasants," which, I am convinced, is one of my very best works. I make this request in the hope that you will grant the wish of the Berlin Academy. The exhibition will naturally assume all responsibility for the safety of the picture, insuring the same.

I will be under great obligations to you if you will grant this request.

With expressions of respect, I remain,

Your obedient servant,

W. LEIBL.

FEBRUARY 11, 1896.

CESARE MACCARI

A CHILD of Siena, where he was born in 1840, but in the real spirit of his life-work a son of Venice, is Maccari. He was a pupil in the academy of his native city, where he won the *Prix de Rome*, and subsequently studied in Florence under Luigi Mussini. At the close of his Roman curriculum he visited Assisi and Venice. The Venetian school powerfully impressed him, and dominated his art. He was first and last devoted to historic painting, giving such splendid results as to draw the eye of Victor Emmanuel, who commissioned him to decorate the ceiling of the royal chapel of the Sudario in Rome. He executed the "Triumph of the Three Graces" in fresco for the Quirinal Palace, and for the mortuary chapel at Campo Verano, a lunette, "Tobias Burying the Dead." Two works, "Melody" and "Fabiola," added much to his fame; the latter belongs to Dupré, of Florence. In 1869 he was honored with gold medals in Siena and Parma; in 1876, in Philadelphia, at the Centennial, and Grand Prize in Turin in 1880. He is a member of the academies in Rome, Genoa, Venice, and Bologna. He also wears the Order of the Italian Crown. His masterpiece is judged to be "The Descent from the Cross," which, for composition, color, and breadth of handling, is one of the most reverent expositions of the tragedy of Golgotha.

RAYMUNDO DE MADRAZO

A DYNASTY of Madrazos may be found in the art history of Spain, with laws of hereditary sceptreship. For more than a hundred years the brush has passed from father to son. It has been the fancy of Eugène Montrosier to sketch in speech the original atelier of Madrazo the First. With a slight paraphrasing it follows : "I see the existence of this enthusiast of the unknown, this seeker of the golden fleece, wandering, as chance directed, with his knapsack on his back, supping on a crust of bread dipped in the brook, sleeping under the stars 'in God's inn,' soothing his distress with a song or a kiss blown from the fingers' ends of the señora leaning from her window, who blushes redder than the pink that is fastened in her black tresses. We would like to describe his rest at the turn of the road, the easel placed, the canvas taken from the box, the colors extracted from the tubes, and the quick sketch made, expressing in a vivid manner the emotions felt. Then the happy chance encounter; a peasant going to town offers the dusty, tired pedestrian a place in his cart, and there is picturesque conversation or observations on things seen and appreciated differently, with warmth of words and eloquent gestures and a ripple of laughter like beads falling from a broken necklace."

José de Madrazo had two sons—Federico and Luis ; Federico, in his turn, also had two sons—Raymundo and Ricardo. The subject of this monograph was born in Rome in 1841, and baptized in St. Peter's. It is said that the priest of the parish initiated him into secrets of painting by allowing him to copy the pictures that were in the sacristy of the church. He received instruction from his father, who died in 1859, as the head of the Madrid Academy. He was also a pupil, in Paris, under Winterhalter, a notable exploiter in portraiture, *genre*, and history. While Ricardo Madrazo, his younger brother, has achieved a position quite his own, there is but one Madrazo who is recognized as the head of the succession in the family, and that upon logical premises established by himself. In 1878 he received for his work at the Salon a first-class medal and the ribbon of the Legion of Honor. Up to that date he had not appeared in any exhibition. He decorated the palace of the Queen of

Spain in the Champs Elysées. "M. de Madrazo is original because he does not proceed like any of his predecessors, although he knows how to make good use of his ancestors. He speaks a new language that has a rhythm of its own, a spontaneous cadence, a generous flavor." In spite of his residence there, and his intimacy with Fortuny, Rico, and Zamacois, he has never become a Parisian. He has the pleasing sensation of being claimed equally by France and Spain. Not unoften the dispute waxes hot, and his artistic indentity becomes the ground of combat. The voluble, flaunting banners that vex the air afford diversion, and beget no fear in the heart of Raymundo de Madrazo. He has permanently impressed his students, variously uttered his aims as a modernist of power, and charmingly invested his life in his friends.

JEAN LOUIS ERNEST MEISSONIER

WHEN Eugène Montrosier said that all of Meissonier's art is summed up in the following observation, "intelligence and emotion enclosed in a panel the size of a hand," he simply indulged in one of those cameos of speech of which the French are so fond, the passion for which sometimes leads them into a superficial estimate, and a disposition to sneer at their more prosaic, but thorough Dutch neighbors. Meissonier could undoubtedly give to his smallest canvas the reach of leagues and the force of an epic, but his masterpieces were not panels "the size of a hand." Nor was all of his art seen within such confined limitations of space. He was so various, so protean, his play of theme so wide, touching the king at one extreme and the bandit at the other, that he refuses to disclose himself save in the complete review and articulation of his whole career. Certain conditions seemed necessary to stir his ardor and arouse his gifts. He must have reality; after that, environment of a vivid kind; form and color were prerequisites, then the composition that threw those into action. He must have action, no matter what its impulse, motive, or end, whether the monarch in purple or the robber in rags; there must be some guerdon at stake, some prize for the game.

Meissonier's idea of repose is a march between two battles, a breathing space by the fire, the story of the day's fight under telling, and valor for to-morrow's fight, with hand on sword-hilt. Up to his date French art had reveled in many fields, and excelled in all except the school of the Dutch masters, whom Meissonier sought to rival. He has surpassed those in skill of detail, although he never became their peer in color. He was pronouncedly of the eighteenth rather than of the nineteenth century. Without poetic temperament or large pretensions towards an ideal, he busied himself in projecting creations which, from thorough knowledge of the epoch he would represent, leads us to live with him in the splendors of the past. He would not have you understand that past by its materialism—costume, bric-à-brac, architecture; he goes beyond these, and reveals its very spirit and color. He never forgets his man in building his sphere around him; he is the central motive that first strikes the eye and grasps the intelligence. To speak of Meissonier as a mere miniaturist, who can pack "fifty French guards, very lifelike and very stirring, on a canvas where two cockchafers would be too crowded," is to judge his art by the canon of sheer manipulation; it is to lose sight of the truthfulness and the soul which have dictated his careful execution.

To one who saw and pondered the exhibition of his studies at the Petit Gallery at Paris, in the year following his death, the open page of his secret was read. It was simply conscientious, incessant toil. This series represented years of notation. These walls were filled with many searchings, perpetual efforts to seize vital factors in his themes. His horses were started, under his pencil, at the bone, and built up from fetlock to head with layers of muscle and nerve finely fibred (for you saw the thoroughbred quality of his animal) and perfectly modeled. In this he was a close kinsman to the great Angelo Buonarroti, whose note-book, still to be seen in his house in Florence, shows that he treated the human figure with the same scientific method; hence the ceiling of the Sistine Chapel at Rome swarms with bodies full of vital fire.

Albert Wolff, referring to Meissonier's studies when yet on the walls of his home, says: "We can there read the sincerity and wonderful determination of a man who leaves nothing to chance, who never loses sight of nature, and who makes no account of time when it behooves him to carry on a work to the pitch of perfection which the artist desires. Drawings, painted sketches, statuettes in wax, have been prepared before the final undertaking; it is the scale practice of this inimitable executant before he plays his piece. In this thorough way he has treated the epic of the first Empire in a great number of compositions, of which the most perfect, 'The Retreat from Russia in 1814,' is not merely a masterpiece of composition and execution, but, again, is a grand page of history in limited form." Who can turn down that chapter, without a sense of its unutterable pathos; while the man who "met at last God's thunder" sets the crushed face of his hope toward France?

Montrosier well-nigh matches Meissonier in picturing the event in words: "In a hollow, broken-up road, furrowed with ruts and soaked with half-melted snow, Napoleon advances at a foot-pace on his white horse, followed by his staff. The generals are dejected and depressed, and dare not break the silence that has fallen on him who so often led them to success. They are marching under a dismal sky. As to Napoleon, he has the air of a Titan overwhelmed. Pale, with dim eyes, the mouth contorted with fever, he moves as one in a dream, letting the hand that holds his riding-whip hang down; the legendary grey coat is wrapped around his febrile-shaken body, but seems too large; under the crush that weighs him down he is lessened in size. His marshals follow him, tired out and humiliated, in despair. Ney, however, shows a good front, but Berthier appears stupefied; the others drag along their fatigue and shame. One of them is sleeping in his saddle, rocked by the cadence of his animal's step. In the distance a column fights in full retreat and is lost to view in the foggy horizon. Routed on every side, the route is strewn with bloody vestiges, the halting-places marked by corpses. But the spectator's eyes leave the mass, to return to that figure of Napoleon with the convulsed mask, where all kinds of grief have placed their stigma; to that colossus which a child's hand could overthrow; to the god of yesterday, crumbling to dust under the feet of destiny."

Meissonier first exhibited, in 1836, "The Little Messenger," but attracted indifferent attention until 1840; then passed quickly into the chamber of renown. He was made Chevalier of the Legion of Honor in 1846, an Officer in 1856, Member of the Institute in 1861, Commander of the Legion of Honor in 1867, Grand Officer in 1878.

He died January 31, 1891. He stood alone in his place; unyielding in his demands upon himself, he would not shift his convictions at the mandate of others. Severely reviewed, the centre of much tumult among the small populations that live beneath precedents and devoutly follow the leadings of some consecrated clique, he serenely held on his course. No dealer dared to tempt him; the rich patron could not juggle with his judgment; the wizard's wand of gold, that has touched into servility so many artists, found him always erect and content. He painted only as his conscientiousness dictated. His house of life was sunlit, with broad verandas toward the south and wide eastern gables. One day Death passed by, going westward, and took him beyond the setting sun, through the portals of immortality.

ADOLF FREDERIC ERDMANN MENZEL

A SERIES of pen-and-ink drawings called "Artist's Pilgrimage" discovered Menzel to the world. These were followed by a cycle of scenes lithographed from the history of Brandenburg. He illustrated Kugler's "Frederick the Great" and the *édition de luxe* of the king's own works. These commissions opened his mind to the magnificence of that reign, and led him to the production of a succession of pictures disclosing its character. These were eminently realistic, combining exceeding skill in the treatment of details, with splendid coloration.

Up to his fortieth year he had celebrated the glorified past of his country. His coronation picture set the seal to the series, which is more than a conventional review of ceremonies, the traditional handling of a court event, but a work of art in that intimate and august sense that gives to Menzel the dignity of a revelator. When he had signed that canvas he went out into the street to be thereafter the apostle of humanity, the friend of those masses who strive and cry, laugh and mourn under the palpitating strain of life. Coming to Paris, he was fascinated by Meissonier; the feeling was mutual. He painted the portrait of the *genreist*. The intimacy settled into a permanent fellowship, and as Menzel could not speak a word of French nor Meissonier a word of German, the two formed an interesting pair to watch in the Salon and elsewhere. Their communications were in dramatic signs. Meissonier's crisp, demonstrative *staccato* of speech and gesture was looked upon by his German comrade with perfect understanding and entire satisfaction. He has been professor since 1856, when he received the great gold medal of the Berlin Academy, of which he was constituted a member. Member also of the academies of Vienna and Munich and of the Société Belge des Aquarellistes. He entered the Legion of Honor, Paris, 1867; the Order pour le Mérite, 1870, and was knighted by the Bavarian Order of St. Michael.

He was born at Breslau, December 8, 1815. In Paris his representations of contemporary life proclaimed him a pioneer there, as he had been in Germany. He was acclaimed with enthusiasm, one panegyrist asserting that "Menzel combined all the qualities of which other men of talent merely possessed fragments separately apportioned among them." He was self-taught, tarrying but a brief time, in 1833, in the Academy of Berlin.

He has stepped aside twice from his canvas to work in fresco. These passages of effort may be seen in the interiors of the churches of Innsbruck and Salzbourg. Émile Michel, in the *Revue des Deux Mondes*, December, 1877, records this word of praise: "Above, vividly lighted, are white walls, pictures and altars resplendent with gilding; then, by insensible degrees, the light decreases, candles burn in a mysterious and lukewarm shade, and below are some faithful ones, absorbed in their prayers, with an expression of silence and deep meditation. In place of the heavy pretentiousness, which too often we have pointed out in the works of German painters, we find here a true artist, full of tact and taste, of elegance and easy grace, who would worthily sustain all comparisons with the best of our French masters."

GÉZA VON MESZÖLY

A HUNGARIAN landscape painter, who studied in Munich, but has transcended the old traditions of that school in his development, and was one of the results of the German Renaissance. He touches his work with pictorial charm, lucid warmth, and poetic fragrance. The scale of his production was not wide, but he moved within it in a calm, reposeful fashion. He took congenial and familiar scenes to shift them in the differentiated lights of the day or tones of the seasons. The shores of Platten Lake held his affectionate consideration. We see the "Fishermen's Huts" there (in the Pesth Museum), the "Twilight Hour," and "Lake Platten, with Fowls." The "Water Carrier on the Banks of the Theiss" was painted in 1885. He was medaled at Munich, 1883.

FRANÇOIS PAOLO MICHETTI

IN the northern part of Italy, central between what were formerly papal states and the shores of the Adriatic, lie three portions of what was once the kingdom of Naples, each of which bore the name of Abruzzo, collectively registered Abruzzi. It is a region seldom visited by tourists, although offering a wild, picturesque mass of mountains and forests, interluded with fat pastures, lakes, and torrent-like rivers. The natives of these highlands give their time chiefly to tending flocks of sheep. During the winter season they descend into the plains; a few at Christmas even stroll to Naples or as far as Rome to sing simple carols and pick up centesimi. This Italian nomadic life charmed the pencil of Signor Michetti, a Neapolitan artist of rare power, who has persistently scorned the merchandise side of art. Years ago we saw one of his earliest examples, called the "Young Shepherdess of the Abruzzi." A child has fallen asleep on the grass by the forest's edge, while a lamb gently pillows its head on her bosom, watching, as would a dog, with wistful solicitude over her safety. The sturdy figure of the sleeper was beautifully modeled, the attitude having the easy abandon of perfect repose. Both she and her keeper were thrown into bold relief by the contrasting screen of the woods, in the midst of which were visible other members of the fold, gazing in astonishment at the scene before them.

Michetti was born at Chieti, near Naples, 1852, and studied under Dalbono, of that city, later in Paris and London. He has been medaled at Rome, Turin, Florence, and Parma, and is Chevalier of the Order of the Crown of Italy. His father was a day laborer, whom he lost in his youth. A gentleman of position became protector to the orphan boy and gave him advantages. In 1876 he returned to the neighborhood of his birthplace, and settled among the Abruzzi, in Francavilla, close to the Adriatic. Here he lived, surrounded by old pictures in the heart of the vigorous life of the Italian peasantry. In 1877 he painted his celebrated "Corpus Domini Procession of Chieti," a picture which is motleyesque in its discharge of color, a very tumult of boisterous rejoicing. The generic meaning of the artist's name is defined here—"Michetti": "splendid materials, dazzling flesh tones, conflicting hues set with intention beside each other." Everything in this canvas bubbles with laughter—every tint of the prism, every face, every flower and fern spray; above all, the genial sun. Now and then Michetti painted the sea. He was prone to take the meridian hour, when the sultry heat broods on the azure water, showing fishermen standing in it or on the shore, and gayly dressed women, with skirts caught up, searching for mussels; while, in the background, boats are seen with dreaming sails. The Spirit of the Tides sleeps, barely breathing in liquid murmurs that fall and faint against the gates of Capri.

Again, the artist sends forth a moonrise over the bay or a flowering hillside on a summer evening, with children in the foreground. Whatever his theme, he is certain of his eye and hand, improvising with precision and dexterity; a Guilleman before the vast organ of nature.

H. HUMPHREY MOORE

A PRESENCE welcomed in the studios of Paris is that of Mr. Moore. He is an American, born in New York City in 1844. Was first a student in the École des Beaux Arts; afterward under Gérôme in Paris, and Fortuny at Madrid. The dominating influence, however, was that of the Spanish rather than French school. He is a figure painter of more than average force. His variations of the subject of the Alhambra have found appreciative buyers. His better-known works are his "Almeh," for which he received a medal at the Philadelphia Centennial; "Moorish Bazaar,"

"The Blind Guitar Player," and "The Moorish Merchant"; the type of this last is from Algiers. His "Almeh" shows consummate skill in composition. "The figure of the swaying and poised woman has the modesty of unconsciousness associated with gayety; the abandon of delight in a voluptuous dance, without the expression or manner of one impure. The dance, or, rather, body-swaying of the 'Almeh,' is located in one of the gorgeous halls of the Alhambra, frescoed in the intricate and dreamy harmony of Moresque decorations; over the floor is spread a carpet rich in warm hues. The attitude of the girl leaves the body semi-nude, and while correct in point of costume, is contrived with consummate judgment for effect in color."

From the studio of Gérôme he turned to that of Fortuny, who wielded the more powerful sceptre over his mind, giving to his work a dash and sparkle which were hitherto wanting. Subsequently he surrendered to the sway of Japanese art, in common with the leading impressionists of the time. His studies in shining reds and yellows have been highly priced on account of their exceeding popularity with American buyers.

DOMENICO MORELLI

A BIBLICAL painter of unique personality was Domenico Morelli. He broke at the start with the reigning powers in that particular branch of Italian art, in the end attaining a mastery and founding a school of his own. He was quite the pattern for such headship: fiery, yet reserved; haughty, independent, and radical. The young men deserted other teachers for his atelier, where he taught them loyalty to the radiant integrity of sun and sea. Among these was Paolo Michetti, whom he counted his prize pupil. Morelli was recognized when young, and sent by the Neapolitan government to Rome. He was placed under the tuition of Prof. Camillo Guerra, but was more influenced by Filippo Palizzi. During a second term at Rome he studied with Overbeck, concluding his preparatory monitions by an extended tour through the art centers of England, France, Germany, Belgium, and Holland. He won first prize at Naples in 1855, the gold medals at Paris in 1861 and 1867, and has been admitted to the Academy of St. Fernando, Madrid, of Fine Arts, Naples, and all the academies throughout Italy. He is Commander of the orders of St. Maurice and St. Lazarus, of the Crown of Italy, and is Cavalier of the Order of Civil Merit of Savoy. His more significant works are: "Cesare Borgia at the Siege of Capua," "Christian Martyrs" (in the Gallery of Capo di Monte), "The Assumption" (in the Royal Chapel at Naples), "Madonna and Child" (in the Church of Castellina), which has been most favorably criticised by Prof. Villari ; a "Christ," painted for Verdi, the composer. At the Paris Exposition in 1878 he showed "The Temptation of St. Anthony," gaining universal sympathy for the saint. His single panel of "A Woman Seated," in Mr. Stewart's group of pictures, is a marked note of clear expression. He was a friend of Fortuny's, upon whose recommendation this drawing was purchased.

GIUSEPPE DE NITTIS

A NOBLE mission was that of Mr. William H. Stewart, who went into the realm of unknown artists on tours of discovery. He had an eye for gifts *in embryo*, and, among others, may be said to have developed de Nittis, whose native place was the town of Barletta, several leagues distant from the battlefield of Cannes. The family was of Spanish origin, and settled in the Sicilies in the eighteenth century. They carried the name of Velasquez. Death took his father and mother when he was very young. At the age of twelve he came to Naples, and at sixteen produced landscapes directly inspired by Nature. His brother bought him a box of colors, those marvelous colors hidden in the white ray, which the prism unweaves. De Nittis gave a brief session to Professor Dattoli, another to the Neapolitan School of Fine Arts, and then swiftly returned to the breast of Nature. After two years of wandering he came back from the fields with a collection of sketches that imperiously took hold of the public and were discusssd in cafés and on street corners. Entering the Museum of Naples, the spell of the old masters fell like dew upon his brain. He tells us that it was from these and Nature in the neighborhood that he gained all his training. He came to Paris to eat the crusts of poverty, not knowing a verb in the language of the city. A fellow-countryman presented him to Brandon, who introduced him to Gérôme, who introduced him to Meissonier. Doors were now opened to this predestined sorcerer. His dauntless, searching, sensitive spirit challenged the stiff posings of David and the classicists of his paternity. He took the people in the streets of Paris off their guard, and caught the crowds *en route*. The "Place des Pyramids" and the view of the "Pont Royal" are superb studies, illustrative of his method. These are exquisitely atmosphered ; the vibrating mist, the shifting, curling smoke, through which graceful figures appear and then vanish, show him as a veritable victor in confronting the subtle street phases of Parisian life. He rejoiced in the "Bois" and in the "Champs Elysées "; he was held by the masses that throbbed and surged between the Arc de Triomphe and the Obelisk.

He loved the feathery blooms of the chestnuts, and the disks of delightful color let into the grass.

Émile Blémont thus characterizes him : "Impressionist in conception, de Nittis is a harmonist in execution ; the unity of the work comes from the unity of the idea. His compositions are as simple as the day and as complex as life. The sun awakens and accentuates the tones, warming and impregnating them with purple and gold, whilst the shadow, calming the brilliancy, softens the contrasts, absorbs the reflections, thus forming by its darker tones the bass of the symphony, vaguely lulling the dark blues and twilight violets of the outlines. And it is as true as it is charming. The effect corresponds exactly to the mathematical bearings of luminous vibrations, to the law of opalescent centers dividing the light into warm tints, which they transmit, and cold tints, that are reflected ; the law of complementary colors, mutually magnified by their opposition ; and the law of collateral colors, where the stronger decompose and partially absorb the feebler. Such an art as this is full of perils. What exactness of sight and delicacy of touch are necessary! But where the science of de Nittis might hesitate, his taste guides him surely; his style is always simple and large. It is certain that since the fifteenth century, art has known the charm of bluish shadows and tempered horizons ; but it is only lately that they have really understood and expressed how much there is of air and sky that is always mingled with terrestrial sights. To perfect and keep himself fresh, de Nittis spares neither time nor trouble. Vivacious, alert, of medium height and well built, the features finely cut, with an intense and slightly concentrated glance, the face remarkably mobile, brown hair and beard, with golden reflections, he is always in movement, always in quest of new fields and unknown sources. Indefatigable, he paints with ardor streets and woods, landscapes of grass and landscapes of stone, wheat-fields, racecourses, earth and water, the Parisian drawing-room toilets and the lone dreariness of a ragged old woman on the banks of the Thames. In an enormous box, with compartments and grooves, he keeps numberless sketches of all sorts. One of the most curious is a study of the sky, done in less than an hour in answer to a challenge of Gérôme and Boulanger. In the infinite azure floats, like white fleece, some wandering vapor ; there is nothing else, and the effect is prodigious. It is Shelley's cloud transposed ; the painter has modeled the impalpable. As he varies his subjects so he varies his processes.

"It was quite late when he specially devoted himself to drawing, but the really great passion of de Nittis is the pastel. If he loses the intense transparency of oil colors, he gains a wonderful rapidity of execution, outlines drawn and colored at a stroke, tones deliciously modeled, and shadows of a strange softness ; he gains that marvelously misty envelopment that yields the golden dust of a sun's ray, the velvet of a ripe fruit, the down of flowering carnations, the haze of the horizon's air, diffused light, atmosphere, and perspective. His *chef-d'œuvre* in this style is the portrait of a woman exhibited in 1882. He passed through impressionism without lingering or losing himself, only keeping a flower of white light with a bit of thread fallen from the scarf of Iris."

He was medaled in Paris—third class, 1876 ; first class, 1878 ; Legion of Honor in the same year. His "Road from Naples to Brindisi" was the chief centre of interest for the Salon of 1872. Of this M. Montaignac thoughtfully says: "An evolution was going on ; painters were trying to free themselves from black and from bitumen ; there was a marked tendency toward the sun—a real sun—not made by black or white ; de Nittis's 'Brindisi Road' appeared. The picture was at the same time a proof and a lesson ; it showed to what point the power of color could be carried without turning things black ; it taught the process to those who were seeking for it."

De Nittis died at St. Germain in 1884. Gérôme, Meissonier, Manet, were the masters whom he welcomed last. While they undoubtedly had a share in the artistic moulding of his individuality, there came a time when but feeble trace of them could be discerned. The maturing soul of the painter had caught higher visions, and was unrestful until these came down to dwell with him.

ALFRED PARSONS

A HEART familiar with the sun beats in the breast of Mr. Alfred Parsons, coloring his art and his life with a golden hue touched with crimson. Mr. Henry James calls him "the painter of happy England," and further exploits his style as one easily ministering to the "quietest complacency" of that self-centred nation. He says Mr. Parsons is "doubtless clever enough to paint rawness when he must, but he has an irrepressible sense of ripeness. Half the ripeness of England, half the religion, one might almost say, is in its gardens ; they are truly pious foundations." Recall Mr. Alfred Austin's book on "The Garden that I Love," the original of which spreads its beauty round the Dower-house of Goddington in Kent. Mr. Parsons has shown us the English passion for flowers, as a protest against the greyness of their climate. He has looked over many walls, gone with observing leisure down many alleyways of hawthorn and boxwood, and caught the fragrant swing of their organized revels of color. Here is one picture for the verbal setting of which we are indebted to Mr. James : "A corner of an old, tumbled-up place in Wiltshire, where many things have come and gone, represents that moment of transition in which contrast is so vivid as to make it more dramatic than many plays; the very youngest throb of spring, with the brown slope of the foreground coming back to consciousness in pale lemon-colored patches, and on the top of the hill, against the still cold sky, the equally delicate forms of the wintry trees. By the time these forms have thickened, the expanses of daffodil will have become a mass of bluebells. All his daffodil pictures have a rare loveliness, but especially those that deal also with the earlier fruit blossom, the young plum trees in Berkshire orchards. Here the air is faintly pink, and the painter makes us feel the little *blow* in the thin blue sky. In every touch of nature that he communicates to us we feel something of the thrill of the whole; we feel the innumerable relations, the possible variations of the particular objects. We walk with him on a firm earth; we taste the tone of the air, and seem to take nature and the climate and all the complicated conditions by their big general hand. The painter's manner, in short, is one with the study of things; his talent is a part of their truth."

He was born in England, 1821. The larger part of his life has been passed in the city of New York and in regions neighboring the metropolis, where he has noted many themes. He is a famed illustrator of books and magazines. In 1860 he was elected an Associate of the National Academy; he is a Member of the Artists' Fund Society and of the Society of Painters in Water Colors. He sent in 1876 to the Water Color Society, "Salem"; in 1877, "November"; in 1878, "Gravesend Bay." His mother-land may still claim him, although he has given the larger share of his years to the United States. He has never lost her inspirations. While following the processional of her seasons, reflecting every phase and tint of her springtides, summer, autumn, and winter moods, he has given to her more than she has bestowed upon him.

AUGUST VON PETTENKOFEN

AN ARTIST rightfully resents comparison, even when it bears the cup of praise, choosing rather to stand on foundations of his own building than to rest on those of another. Professor Pettenkofen has been called the Austrian Meissonier. He does not need that title to carry prestige to his name. He was born in Vienna in 1823; studied at the academy there, but was seriously discontented with the tuition proffered. He sought better instruction in the productions of Wouvermans and Van de Velde. Afar off he heard rumors of a band of seekers—Troyon, Rousseau, Daubigny in Paris, of Leys and Stevens in Belgium, and preened his wings for flight beyond the bounds of the German-Austrian school. Meantime he was compelled to respond to the regulation conscription, and was drafted into the army of Francis Joseph. He rose rapidly from the ranks, and was promoted to the grade of captain. But the mission of arms could not adequately voice his dreams. So soon as his term of service ended he returned to the brush, to become the representative painter of Austria. He turned to his experiences as captain for a field of suggestion, and was soon pouring forth a mass of incidents from the army and its unruly Hungarian contingent that have historical verity. He craved the company of the group of searchers whose renown had reached him in Vienna, and turned towards Paris, where he completed his transition from ossified to living *genre* work. He took under his arm two sketches, "The Spy" and "Marauders Dividing Booty," the last of which found a purchaser in Sir Richard Wallace. He has multiplied the scenes of his army life, and wrought groups from the villages of Bohemia and Hungary. Mr. Van Cuyck was so fascinated with his "Marauders" that he requested the privilege of two pictures from the artist—"Scene After a Duel" and "Hungarian Volunteers." The last was sold to M. Roné, who exhibited it at the Cercle de l'Union Artistique. Mr. Van Cuyck so bitterly regretted its loss that he repurchased it, saying that only death should take it from his possession. It was on the value of this canvas that Professor Pettenkofen received a decoration from the Emperor of Austria, who saw it at Vienna in 1873. His "Austrian Cavaliers Passing a Ford" was sold to the Frankfort Museum. In the yearly exhibition at Vienna in 1876 he displayed his most remarkable picture, "A Market Scene in Hungary." He is Chevalier of the Order of the Crown of Oak.

CHARLES HENRI PILLE

A PEASANT in the character of his presence, this artist is none the less a refined and observant gentleman, who has brought to his easel a sagacious mind under the control of noble aims. He impresses by his direct simplicity of motive and poetic purity, combining firmness of technique with the intimacy and vital freshness of his subjects. His personal equation is expressed in fundamental honesty, frankness, repose, translucence ; the man has ruled the artist, producing compositions of truth and of style; which is "a manner of right seeing and true doing." Henri Pille is gifted with a remarkable memory. It is recited of him by a friend who had attended the theatre in his company, that the next day he saw him, while delivering reflections on the intrigues and whole effect of the play, design with rigorous exactness the costumes of the actors in their least details, indicating the colors and the shades. He exhibited in the Salon of 1870 "Sancho Recounting his Exploits to the Duchess"; in 1872, "Autumn"; in 1873, "Matrimonial Accord"; in 1875, "Market at Antwerp" and "Old Clothes"; in 1876, "The Morning Interview, Intemperance and Sobriety."

GEORGE JOHN PINWELL

AN engraver on wood for illustrated books was the original sphere of this artist. He advanced to water-color themes, and at once solicited the consideration of connoisseurs. He was elected an Associate of the Society of Water Colors in 1869, contributing frequently to the exhibitions in Dudley Gallery up to 1871, when he was made a full member, but frail health restrained him from activity after that date. His "Pied Piper of Hamelin," "The Elixir of Love," "The Saracen Maiden," and "The Strolling Player" are his most important examples. There was an atmosphere of pathos in his work. His appeal was to the thoughtful rather than to those who seek qualities of art only on the surface. Pinwell repaid the study of underlying history. He was born in London in 1842, and passed to rest in 1875. His works are rarely seen to-day outside of collections.

ROMAN RIBERA

A PUPIL of Lorenzalez, Ribera was caught in the influences that were set in play by the honest effort of Spain to free herself from conventionalisms, and to look at the world with eyes cleared of mists and untwisted by the strabismus of consecrated precedent. His "Café Chantant" reveals the grasp and brush-work of a master with a fine certainty of characterization. Contemporary life affords Ribera his field. He received honorable mention at the Paris Exposition, 1878, and the gold medal at Barcelona ten years later. He is Fellow of the Royal Academy of Art, Knight of the Order of Isabella, and of the Order of Christo of Portugal.

MARTIN RICO

A GUITAR and a generous bundle of cigarettes could take Rico round the globe. He came to his first knowledge of art through the kindness of a cavalry captain, who taught him to draw. From the trooper he passed to the Madrid Academy, and, as he progressed, made his living by engraving on wood in moments of leisure. With a few jingling coins in his pocket, he would take long excursions through the country, getting upon friendly terms with herdsmen or gypsies, reducing expenses to the minimum, and not unfrequently having to beg his way back to the city. In 1862 he secured the first *Prix de Rome* ever given at Madrid for landscape. The four years' pension carried the privilege of a choice between Rome and Paris. Rico went to Paris. Zamacois introduced him to Daubigny and Meissonier. When his pensionate had expired he was fortunate in finding that prince of patrons, the father of Mr. Julius L. Stewart, the artist, who gave him advancement until, well on his feet, he could march single-file. He was susceptible to the delicate moods of Nature, her restful interludes, her deeps of still skies unvexed by tempests, even undreamed of clouds. His spirit was steeped in light and toned with color. Mr. John C. Van Dyke, in the *Art Review* of December, 1887, says of him : " Entirely different from Rousseau, he did not paint the strong, enduring, storm-tossed trees of the centuries, but rather the soft, delicate foliage of early summer swayed by the slightest breeze or hanging motionless in the heated air. The world of nature seems to have been a sort of dreamland to Rico, for his art was flooded with a 'rapture of repose' that steals over the sunlit streets, the silent water, the nodding trees, and the distant hills. This was his point of view, and when men like Rico put their impressions on canvas, conveying it to others by technical skill, it is rightly called art."

He was the intimate comrade of Fortuny, and was with him in Italy for a longer time than any other friend. His pictures of this period are Fortunesque ; indeed several of his sea pieces, especially those of the Venetian canals and the Bay of Fontarabia, might have been painted by the distinguished Catalonian himself. In others he appears more serene and harmonious than the latter. Richard Muther deems his execution more powerful ; " less marked by spirited stippling, his light gains in intensity and atmospheric refinement what it loses in mocking caprices." Certain market scenes, with a dense crowd of buyers and sellers, are peculiarly spirited, rapid sketches, with a gleaming charm of colors. In 1878 he was medaled at the Salon and endowed with the Cross of the Legion of Honor. In the days of his opulence he does not forget his struggles and the narrow margins of his boyhood, maintaining very simple habits. He travels widely and far for fresh things, and, whether in water colors or oils, so brilliantly speaks as to command the praise of the people and the franchise of the rich. He was personally precious to Fortuny.

ANTON ROMAKO

THIS whole-hearted *genre* painter was born at Atzgersdorf, not far from Vienna, in 1835. He was a pupil of the Vienna Academy and of Rahl, and subsequently resided in Rome. His Italian figure-work is of first rank. He made a permanent success in rendering the child-life of Vienna, and is strongly akin to Knaus in the verity and spirit of his compositions. Medals, 1869 and 1872; Legion of Honor, 1882. His pen-and-ink sketches are of a high order. For him the aim of art was not beauty, but the expression of truth.

C. BARONESS DE ROTHSCHILD

A DISTINGUISHED artist in a family of renown, who paints for her pleasure and that of her friends. She is a member of the Société de Aquarellistes in Paris, and occasionally exhibits, as instanced by the two effective landscapes shown in London in 1875. Her status carries the strength of a professional, although she ranks as an amateur, being unwilling to sell her pictures. The canvas to be seen in this collection was a gift by the artist to a charitable fair held in Paris, and was purchased there by Mr. Stewart.

THÉODORE ROUSSEAU

THERE is one name in the annals of modern French art that must give a thrill of joy and a consciousness of assured satisfaction whenever it is written, whether the pen be in the hand of a venerable *savant* like Albert Wolff, or the merest tyro who takes art for a tonic. The name is the caption of this unworthy monograph. Who has not felt the futility of words in the presence of a great creation? A cliff at sea, whose ledges hew out of the pitiless bulk and green gloom of great billows; passionate hearts "white as snow and tenderer than lilies"; a peak cleaving the air, an eyrie for mountain eagles, and an altar for worship; a sunset trembling on the sky like "a harvest kingdom of red wheat"; an oak by Rousseau, whose roots grip the ribs of earth, whose body gives greeting alike to sun-floods or storms; a Titan unbent by the tread of a thousand years. This artist was the supreme intellectual painter of France, an aspirant for knowledge until the black fog of death dimmed his brain. A glimpse of his method has been given us by M. Alfred Sensier in his book, "Souvenirs sur Théodore Rousseau."

"I went to see him in Indian summer in November. His little house was covered with clematis and nasturtiums. He showed me a whole collection of pictures, sketches, monotint studies, and compositions 'laid in,' which made him ready for twenty years' work. He was beginning his beautiful landscape, 'The Charcoal Burner's Hut,' so luminous and so limpid. He had laid it in with the right general effect at the first painting on a canvas prepared in grey tints, and after having placed his masses of trees and the lines of his landscape, he was taking up, with the delicacy of a miniaturist, the sky and the trunks of the trees, scraping with a palette knife to half the depth of the painting and retouching the masses with imperceptible subtlety. 'It seems to you that I am only caressing my picture, does it not? That I am putting nothing on it but magnetic flourishes? I am trying to proceed like the work of nature itself, by accretions which, brought together or united, become forces, transparent atmospheric effects, into which I put afterward definite accents as upon a woof of neutral value. These accents are to painting what melody is to harmonic bass, and they determine everything, either victory or defeat. The method is of slight importance in these moments when the end is in sight; you may make use of anything, even diabolical conjurings,' he said to me, laughingly, 'and when there is need of it I use a scraper, my thumb, a piece of cuttlebone, or even my brush-handles. They are hard trials, these last moments of the day's work, and I often come from them worn out, but never discouraged.' Then stopping short in his talk, 'Come, let us go for a walk; I will show you a little of the law of growth in nature itself.'"

Rousseau had plunged into nature's centre. His landscapes are laid down on a world the anatomy of which was familiar to him. He is the majestic prophet of solitude, of vast plains and forests, a revealer of moss-grown rocks, in the midst of which he sets his gigantic trees. His favorite was the oak, the primeval wide-branched oak, such as stands in one of his masterpieces—"A Pond."

Plants, trees, and rocks were not forms summarily observed and clumped together in an arbitrary fashion; for him they were beings gifted with a soul, breathing creatures, each one of which had its physiognomy, its individuality, its part to play, and its distinction of being in the great whole of universal nature. He tells us: "By the harmony of air and light, with that of which they are the life and the illumination, I will make you hear the trees moaning beneath the north winds, and the birds calling to their young." He has the attitude of Turgenieff's "Sportsman" toward Nature. Man receives neither love nor hatred at her hands. She looks beyond him with her deep, earnest eyes, because he is an object of complete indifference to her. "The last of thy brothers might vanish off the earth, and not a needle of the pine tree tremble." While this is the philosophical posture of Rousseau's mind, no man has informed nature with deeper moods, reflecting the spirit of the child, whom God has placed before her. In fact, the greatest picture he ever painted lets forth this accordant note. It is called "Le Givre," and is the crown jewel in that marvelous grouping of gems known as the "Walters Collection." What Turner's "Slave Ship" was to the realm of marine art, Rousseau's "Le Givre" is to the realm of landscape. The earth is ridged as from the spasms of an old agony, the grass turned to a hoary green beneath the withering frost; the forest-masses of the background stand at arms while the day dies. Everywhere one reads the shadowy footmarks of sorrows that have journeyed that way, going down into the valley and beyond the hills, pilgrims to a dreaded destiny. There is a tragic memory in the sunset. This canvas is the bitter epic of a soul whom want and the world's scorn were seeking to drive to despair. But the world and want reckoned without knowledge of the man whose patient courage will fight as long as his dust holds together. It is a perpetual satire on Paris that "Le Givre" was carried all day through the streets of the city by Dupré, who failed to find a purchaser, and sold it in the late evening to Baroilhet, the singer, for five hundred francs; who, counting out the sum, said with a sigh, "Paintings will be my ruin in the end"! What changes were wrought by the time Edmond About, in his notes on the artists of the Salon of 1857, wrote these words:

"Théodore Rousseau has been for twenty-five years the first apostle of truth in landscape. He made a breach in the wall of the historic school, which had lost the habit of regarding nature and servilely copied the bad copyists of Poissin. This audacious innovator opened an enormous door by which many others have followed him. He emancipated the landscape painters as Moses formerly liberated the Hebrews *in exitu Israel de Ægypto*. He led them into a land of promise, where the trees had leaves, where the rivers were liquid, where the men and animals were not of wood. On the return of this truant school the young landscapists forced the entrance of the Salon, and it was still Théodore Rousseau who broke down the door. In that time Rousseau occupied the first rank in landscape—above all, as a colorist ; but neither the institute nor the public wished to confess it. His uncontestable talent was contested by all the world. It is only to-day that his reputation is made."

Thirty years have gone since this panegyric was penned, and these years have proved that not a single sentence was overcharged with praise. He was born in Paris, 1812. Pupil of Guillon-Lethière, whose lessons he soon forgot. Chevalier of the Legion of Honor. His adversaries pursued him to the last, and wounded him sorely by neglect and intrigues. The slight put upon him, though chief of the section of the jury at the Universal Exposition of 1867, in his failure to receive the rosette of the Legion, hurt him keenly. In the distribution of official recompenses others were preferred. Among the fragments of letters found at his death was the draft of a protest to the Emperor, which was never sent ; he had torn it asunder and thrown it aside, too proud to make the appeal for justice. A few years after his marriage his wife was seized by madness, and though his friends besought him to put her away in some retreat, he would never consent. Whilst he tended her he became the victim of a brain affection which clouded his end. In 1867, when Rousseau lay dying, a parrot screamed, and his demented wife danced and trilled. He was buried in front of the forests he loved at Barbizon. His friend Millet set up a memorial for him, a simple cross carved upon an unhewn block of sandstone, with tablet of brass engraved " *Théodore Rousseau, Peintre.*"

FERDINAND ROYBET

HE has the right to rival the old Spanish masters on account of the glowing tone with which he has invested his cavaliers of the seventeenth century. Roybet conserves the identity of the historical, but does not sacrifice his pictorial art to it. He has given an accomplished translation of the aspects of the period in which he revels. He was born at Uzès, 1840. Studied at the School of Arts at Lyons. Settled in Paris, 1864. He sent the "Jester of Henry III." to the Paris Salon of 1866, for which he was medaled. He knew how to give environment to his great people, a skill in which the French have pronounced mastership. He presents his superb cavaliers and their ladies, grouped with vivid power within picturesque incidents and surroundings. The formal is charged with vitality, the ceremonious is shaped into plastic expression; hence we have movement and the delight of life. He would not paint unattractive histories; his accurate sense of events and their bearings must needs have the allurement of fascinating episodes. To the large circle to whom he speaks he has proved himself brilliant, original, and sincere. We know that an exhibition of his collected works in Paris, 1890, was the occasion of an enthusiasm which has been rarely aroused by any display in that city of the productions of a single hand.

JAMES SANT

THE "principal painter in ordinary to Her Majesty" is the title which is worn by James Sant. The honor is well bestowed. He was born in London, 1820. A pupil of Varley, who prepared him for the Royal Academy, which he entered at the age of twenty years. Shortly thereafter he found his sphere in the painting of portraits. Among his earlier efforts we have "Samuel," 1853; "Children of the Wood," 1854; "The First Sense of Sorrow," which led to his election as an Associate of the Royal Academy in 1862. Among his circle of sitters we find the Duc d'Aumale; the Lord Bishop of London, whom he painted in 1865; the Queen and the children of the Prince of Wales, 1872. His "Young Whittington" was shown at the Centennial, Philadelphia, 1876; "The Early Post" and "Adversity" at Paris, 1878. Referring to "The Early Post," the *Art Journal*, July, 1875, gives unqualified praise: "Mr. Sant has given us everything in this painting—youth, beauty, life, sympathy, a charming story, and a very pleasant reminiscence of an English country house without our ever having been there. As an example of careful art-work and purity of tone in coloring, this composition of itself is excellent, but as an incident of everyday life depicted on canvas it is one of the best pictures of the Academy."

WILLIAM SMALL

AN English landscape painter residing in London, whose artistic qualities have made him for years a most reliable contributor to the Royal Academy. Whatever he undertook, the result was a picture. It is not a fragmentary effort to catch some transient phase of nature, not an exhibition showing the presence of some clique or school in art, but a whole story from the great book, a beautiful rehearsal of some single song or chapter out of the heart of the world. He demonstrates a well-balanced unity, regard for eminent leaders in landscape, and has caught connections concerning the body of things about him that assert his own right to rank among the best exponents in modern English art. He is a Member of the Institute of Painters in Water Colors. He has gained the patronage of a loyal constituency, who steadily purchase his pictures. He has shown "The Fallen Monarch," "Early Spring," and "The Harvest Field" in water color. In oils, through recent years, he has exhibited "After the Storm," "Highland Harvest House." To the Paris Exposition in 1878 he sent "The Wreck," in oil, and "The Beech-Trees" and "Poplars," in water color. The *Art Journal* of July, 1876, ventures to speak of "The Wreck" as a "noble specimen of grandly painted seascape, certainly one of the masterpieces of the year." There is a marked influence of Constable on his finest examples.

ALFRED STEVENS

A CONJUNCTION of a Belgian and a Frenchman is seen in the massive, broad-shouldered man who stands before us. Perhaps the Belgian strain is the more strongly current in his blood, but of this the critics are not sure; where these are in doubt let angels fear to tread. Alfred Stevens represents health and color in art. His healthfulness is not so intrusive as to be ill bred, for no man has surpassed him in rendering pictures at once solid and refined, graceful and even. He carries a dexterous brush in a large deft hand, and produces what men love to linger over, with a finished style, an elegant execution, and sincere poetic sentiment. His patronage has been powerful from the beginning; honors have come to him with growing significance. He has been medaled in Brussels and Paris, third, second, and first classes; Member of the Legion, in which he attained Commander's place in 1878. Austria, Bavaria, the museums of France, Belgium, Germany, and England give prominent recognition to his name. Born at Brussels, 1828.

JULIUS L. STEWART

A PARISIAN from Philadelphia is the characterization that has been made of this gifted artist and cultured gentleman. He reversed the course of Mr. Humphrey Moore, who went from Gérôme to Fortuny. Mr. Stewart went from the atelier of Zamacois, Fortuny's pupil, to that of Gérôme. His antecedents fitted him for the broadest training, his father, one of the most renowned of modern collectors, giving every advantage to his son. The leading critic of the continent has said: "The earlier original works of Julius Stewart were as brilliant, as colorful, and spirited as if they had come from an easel native to Spain or Italy, but with his advancing powers and his wider social range in Paris his style assumed a more subtle and elegant form; he occupies to-day a unique place as the painter *par excellence* of modern social life in the gay city." His "Five O'Clock Tea" was one of the most refined pictures of the Paris Exposition of 1889. "The Hunt Ball" ("After the Hunt") won him fame on both sides of the sea. It is now owned by the Hon. Franklin Murphy, of Newark.

Mr. Stewart is distinctly a modernist, giving serious weight to every fresh movement in the kingdom of art, ready to discern values in any school that reveals firmer, closer hold on the verities of life and the truths of nature. His advance has been toned by the reflected lights of Gérôme, Madrazo, Zamacols, while at his belt he wears the key which he alone has forged, which he alone can turn. Mr. Stewart received honorable mention in the Paris Salon of 1885; Member of International Jury, Paris Universal Exposition, 1889 *(hors concours)*; medal, Salon, 1890; gold medal, Berlin, 1891; Knight of the Order of Leopold of Belgium, 1894; Knight of the Legion of Honor, 1895; grand gold medal, Berlin, 1896; gold medal, Munich, 1897; Member of Jury of Selection for World's Columbian Exposition, where, in consideration of this honor, he did not compete. In 1895 his "View of Venice" was bought by the German Emperor.

CONSTANT TROYON

THE mastership of Troyon lay in his breadth of technique, harmony of composition, and an intuitive, direct seizure of nature at first hand. It would be a flippant and useless travesty on the man to trace him back to the days when he painted porcelains at Sèvres. He came to the unfolding of his potential self in communion with souls kindred to his own : Théodore Rousseau and Jules Dupré. He was a landscape painter of finished power before his visit to Belgium and Holland, which turned his attention to animal life. Those who have been privileged to study the features of his genius as a landscapist will ever be grateful that he graduated there first. The example in the collection of Mr. Quincy Shaw, of Boston, is quite the highest expression of his ability—a noble, strong handling of surfaces that impress the beholder as having been laid upon foundations of granite. The tree-forms are magnificently built up and buttressed. They recall the sturdy standing of Rembrandt's oaks—as though they were living personalities conquering under the sweep of the north wind and the flails of tempests.

In fact, it was Rembrandt, rather than Paul Potter or Albert Cuyp, who set a broader vital impulse stirring in his blood. In 1859 Troyon painted the picture in the Louvre which displays him at the meridian of his power. "Till then," says Muther, "no animal painter had rendered with such combined strength and actuality the long, heavy gait, the philosophical indifference, and the quiet resignation of cattle ; the poetry of autumnal light and the mist of morning, rising from the earth and veiling the whole land with grey, silvery hues. The deeply furrowed, smoking field makes an undulating ascent, so that one seems to be looking at the horizon over the broad face of the earth. A primitive Homeric feeling rests over it. What places Troyon far above the old painters is his fundamental power as a landscapist, a power unequaled except in Rousseau. His 'Cow Scratching Herself' and his 'Return to the Farm' will be counted amongst the most forceful animal pictures of all ages."

It was in 1847 that he astonished the Salon with a cattle piece so strong in color and of such vivid realism that he established his fame at a stroke. His art is penetrated with poetry, the rustic poetry of out-of-doors on a clear-minded day ; a poetry that sweeps with its vision the fields, the herds, the dogs, the Keeper, the grass, flowers, every flame-like spire and leaf in the woods ; while arching all is the great sky, like a vast chalice of sapphire overturned, from the rim of which foaming clouds slowly drop and drift. Troyon sent sixty masterpieces to the Salon between the years 1823 and 1865. In this last year a shadow fell on his easel, and death turned a renowned career into a renowned memory. Mr. William Henry Howe (himself a strong painter of animals), in "Modern French Masters," has this estimate, which is an up-to-date type of intelligent regard and differentiation touching Troyon: "Potter, as an animal painter, was never the equal of Troyon. He could paint isolated objects with harsh truth, but he never could gain the whole, the *ensemble* of things, as compared with Troyon. He could paint cowhides and cow anatomy, but he never could paint cow life. Albert Cuyp could give the truth of a cow's skeleton, the rack of bones and members, with exceptional force, but Troyon, in painting cows—the clumsy, wet-nosed, heavy-breathing bovine—was vastly his superior. Again, Landseer could humanize dogs and other animals, giving them a sentiment quite opposite to their nature, but Troyon never distorted or sentimentalized in any such way. He told the truth. It has been said that he was the most sympathetic painter of this century. It may be added that in the painting of animals and their homes he was the greatest painter of this or any other century."

Hamerton's "Contemporary French Painters" gives a kindred estimate: "In the 'Oxen Going to Work' we have a page of rustic description as good as anything in literature—of fresh and misty morning air, of rough, illimitable land, of mighty oxen marching slowly to their toil! Who that has seen these creatures work can be indifferent to the steadfast grandeur of their nature? They have no petulance, no hurry, no nervous excitability; but they will bear the yoke upon their necks and the thongs about their horns, and push forward without flinching from sunrise until dusk."

He was ever seeking new themes, and greeted with delight any variation from the average body-colors of his friends on the turf. Upon one occasion he was saluted with mocking hilarity in the midst of neighbors, when he tied up to paint a cow of magnificent tawny tone. She was an animal, in their judgment, of but little value. "This gentleman," they said, "has chosen to represent in his picture the only worthless creature there is in the whole pasture. Why, she is being fattened for the butcher!"

How suggestive "the point of view" becomes under the light of this incident. Troyon saw rare color and splendid form. The farmers saw only a poor milk-giver. Each from his own logical outlook was right. Troyon never married, devoting himself to his mother and his art. She established, as a memorial of her son, "The Troyon Prize" for students in animal life. His massive frame, dissolved in dust, lies in the old historic Montmarte Cemetery of Paris, but surely he is with Rousseau.

JOSEPH HENRI FRANÇOIS VAN LERIUS

BORN at Boom, near Antwerp, 1823; passed outward, 1876. A noble teacher of the art he finely illustrated. He was early inclined to his professional career. Studied in the Academy of Brussels, where his rapid development astonished the masters. He was sent, at the expense of his native village, to the academy at Antwerp, entering at the age of fifteen. Here he took all prizes, and so captured the interest of the president, Baron Wappers, that he took him into his own studio as an assistant. His first picture was a scene from Sir Walter Scott's "Kenilworth"—an interview between "Leicester and Amy Robsart." This was followed by "Milton Dictating Paradise Lost to his Daughter." In 1848 he exhibited at the Brussels Exposition a picture for which he was awarded the gold medal. "Joan of Arc" was shown in 1860, the year of his appointment as Professor of Painting in Antwerp Museum. The incident on which the work was based is said to have occurred when La Pucelle was in command of the army at the siege of Paris. The tradition is, that upon going the rounds of the camp, as was her custom, she came upon soldiers carousing with followers of the army. Her indignation was so great that she delivered a blow of menace on the air with such violence that the miraculous sword, which had been sent her from Fiertoes, was broken in two. The dramatic pose of Joan's figure is as superb as the attitudes of the men and women are abject and affrighted. For this work Van Lerius was medaled with gold in Amsterdam, and elected to an honorary membership in the Academy. At the International Exposition at Munich in 1869 he exhibited a dramatic work representing a maiden plunging headlong from her chamber window to escape dishonor. Among his later efforts were "The First-Born," bought by Queen Victoria; "Volupté et Dénouement," purchased by Prince Saxe-Coburg of Gotha. In 1877 the city of Antwerp bought the "Lady Godiva."

ÉMILE VAN MARCKE

HIS father had been a pupil of Watelet, and was favorably known in Germany as a landscape painter. His mother, who was French, was an artist of flowers, receiving a medal at the yearly salon where she exhibited. Émile was their only son. It was at the Liege drawing school that he took up his first studies. Here he carried off all the prizes, but was restrained from vanity by the thorough counsels of his father and mother. He married early the daughter of M. L. Robert, for a long period connected with the Sèvres manufactory, and who, at the death of Regnault, became chief director. Here he secured a position for his son-in-law, who seriously began upon his work of decorating on glazes, and followed it for nine years. He executed landscapes relieved by animal forms. Several large-sized pieces on *pâte tendre* were offered as gifts to sovereigns; those presented to the Queen of Holland were of unusual beauty. Troyon, whose mother lived at Sèvres, visited her frequently, and was attracted to Van Marcke, to whom he offered instruction. The relation became confidential, and to the young artist the realization of his ambition. His first canvas was a success, but the critics, instead of seeing Van Marcke in it, saw Troyon. For many years this proved a limitation on him in the judgment of the public. The formula was very simple through which he was compromised and was disbarred from his rightful estate.

Those who liked his painting (and they were numerous) could find no better compliment to offer him than to say : "It is worthy of Troyon." Those who desired to underrate his work, whilst, however, recognizing his incontestable qualities, said : "Without doubt it is good, but it is only a reflection, and I prefer the original." When Troyon died in 1865, the art critics proffered sympathy to Van Marcke, who, having no longer his accustomed counselor, would be much embarrassed. As usual, the critics were wrong; the exact reverse resulted, and the artist achieved his personality. Normandy was his chosen sketching ground, where he purchased a farm and successfully speculated in raising herds of fat cattle. He painted these as lost in endless content, gravely chewing the cud of comfort, standing hoof-deep in lush grasses under the quietude of wide-spreading heavens. He placed his animals away from the reach of distempered weather, enclosing them in atmospheres so serene as to give a heavy dewfall to pasture lands. He died in 1891, and left no successor. His career was a splendid culmination. The greatest success recorded for such an event was in the sale of his effects. An increasing appreciation marks his work.

DANIEL VIÈRGE URRABIETA

THE art of illustration is that graphic representation which "sets forth in a clear manner those aspects of scenes and incidents that no verbal discription, however elaborate, can give." While the art is ancient, its evolution and application may be said to be modern—and ours by right of conquest. As the pioneer of that victory stands Vièrge, who has been called the "father of modern illustration." He has stood unrivaled for a quarter of a century, and every stroke of his stylus is considered the production of a master. Gustave Flaubert compares the man of genius to a powerful horse tortured by the cruel spur and bit of routine, who, nevertheless, forges forward, bearing along with him his reluctant rider—humanity. Vièrge has been the witness of his own apotheosis and the development of his art to the point of picturing living people in living attitudes, rendering through the simple media of black and white the very atmosphere and even hues of color. August F. Jaccaci has well defined his peculiar trend and preëminent gift :

"Vièrge is a realist in that he is a worshiper of truth ; but realist is a misleading epithet, embracing as many sins as virtues. Far from the low realism of the commonplace and nastiness is that realism of Vièrge which beautifies all that it feeds upon, because it delights in dwelling on those elements of beauty and goodness existing latent or revealed in all things. Perhaps the most personal, and thus the most strongly felt, trait of Vièrge is his faculty of imparting a sort of heroic character—all his own—to his representations of reality. It seems as if there is more of the Moor than of the Spaniard in his nature, as if his work was a revelation of that fine race that knows how to drape itself in a rag, and on whose lips the honey of beautiful verses is born of a ray of sunlight. But his art is as naturally alert as it is dignified."

Under a stroke of paralysis that smote his right side, he has been compelled to teach his left hand the craft of its brother. This slow process has at last resulted in satisfactory skill. He is not more than in life's prime, and gives pledge of deepening the fountains of his inspiration. The field for the gifted illustrator is contemporaneous with every phase and fact of life. The craving of the multitude is not for such knowledge of events as comes from a serious study of their rise and evolution, a philosophical searching into the root-bed of historic growths ; but a swift comprehension of the speech and deeds of mankind pictorially presented ; a brilliant summary of the chapters humanity writes under the daily goings of the sun. The man who leads the art of illustration in these primal expressions must take large space on the horizon of the future.

ANTOINE VOLLON

WHEN the Professor of Art History in the University of Breslau was asked his judgment of Vollon, he made reply : "The greatest painter of still life in the century." Again, Vollon has been termed "the painter's painter," so richly defined, so preciously pedantic is this artist.

He was born in 1833 at Lyons, and is a pupil of Ribot. He was at first rejected by the Salon, but with unfailing courage knocked again and again against the clamps of professional stupidity. These were broken in 1865, when he was awarded a medal. In 1868 and 1869 came other medals ; in 1878 one of the first class. It was in this year that the officership of the Legion of Honor fell to him. A study of two fish won the red ribbon ; this picture was purchased by the government, and is in the Luxembourg. In 1897 he was elected a Member of the Institute of France. He has founded a school of painting in which still life is raised to the dignity of history. The accessories to his themes are as finely handled as the propositions. "He paints dead saltwater fish like Abraham Van Beyeren ; grapes and crystal goblets like Davids de Heem, dead game like Frans Snyders." He is the master in the representation of freshly gathered flowers, crisp vegetables, copper kettles, weapons, and suits of armor. With breadth of treatment he obtains equally power of realization. Vollon amazed everybody at the Salon of 1876 with a single life-sized female figure, "A Fisher Girl of Dieppe," painted with exceeding power.

In 1877 he appeared again in a new phase. Instead of pots, kettles, old armor, or jeweled glass filled with half-transparent fruits, he treats a landscape subject. It is a dreary reach of country, with long sweep of road, extending afar into the horizon, upon which a horseman is galloping ; a few houses at the side, giving human touch to the expanse. The chief values are found in the sky, where squadrons of clouds are scurrying before a furious wind, tumbling and torn. The blast, that whips the flying vapors, twists at the traveler's cloak, who, with bent head, seeks to gain his goal. It is a weird, impressive canvas, all the more so because a distinct departure from the path the artist is accustomed to tread. To be so versatile carries a temptation to superficiality, to which artists have not unfrequently yielded. Vollon never is less than perfect in the patient technique with which he unfolds and accents his theme.

OTTO WEBER

A GERMAN artist, whose rank is in the class with the Bonheurs. He was born at Berlin, and killed in the Franco-Prussian war of 1870. In his native city he was under Steffeck, and in Paris a pupil of the great Couture. For a number of years his studio was in Milan. His medals came in the years 1864 and 1869. The range of his subjects was wide ; in each example he manifested an equal faculty for successful treatment. It is unusual to find a Teutonic artist who can quickly adjust his canvas to such marked variations of expression. His "Ox Team," "The Deer Quarry," "Fête in Brittany," and "The Haygathering" show plastic power in an unusual degree. Whether handling figures or landscapes, he was equally happy.

Two of his pictures are in the Luxembourg. Some years ago he exhibited in London, Suffolk Street Gallery, a work which firmly settled his grasp upon English regard. The scene represented Bavarian peasants bringing their cattle down from the mountains. In ease of manipulation, living postures, keen accuracy, supreme excellence of landscape, ranging from green valleys to mountain-peaks covered with snow, it was an example worthy of Troyon.

EDUARDO ZAMACOÏS

A DAWN suddenly fading on the forehead of heaven ; a summer-tide swiftly stemmed and frozen; a warrior, with his combat just fairly on, stricken down; a singer, his voice shattered into silence, while the sweeter half of the strain is yet in his soul. Thus Death lost to us Regnault, Fortuny, and Zamacoïs. He was born at Bilboa in 1840 ; was trained in Paris under Meissonier; entered the Salon in 1863, when he startled the art public with the brilliancy of a meteor. He was medaled in 1867. His first picture was the "Enlisting of Cervantes." In 1864 he set forth the "Conscripts in Spain" ; in 1866, "The Entrance of the Toreros" (painted in part by Vibert); in 1870, his remarkable canvas, "The Education of a Prince."

Eugene Benson's monograph upon Zamacoïs carries the force of dramatic fervor: "Zamacoïs, with a manner almost as perfect as Meissonier's, is a satirist; he is a man of wit. I should suggest the form and substance of his works as a painter by saying that he has done what Browning did as a poet when he wrote the 'Soliloquy of the Spanish Cloister.' . . . It is manifest that Zamacoïs admires Molière; that he appreciates the picturesque side of Victor Hugo's genius. Zamacoïs does with form and color what Tennyson does with words—that is to say, he combines them in a studied and jeweled style, to express his pleasure in intense and brilliant things. But he has wit, and no one would accuse Tennyson of that Gallic trait. Therefore, to make you acquainted with Zamacoïs, I must say he has a suspicion of malice that must be delightful to the compatriots of Voltaire; that he is bold and positive in his conceptions and fine and elaborate in his expressions.

"His color was pure and intense, his style finished and fine. It was not enough for him to make his point, but he must also make it as perfectly and completely as he possibly could. Like Molière, with whose genius that of Zamacoïs displays a decided affinity, the effect of the artist's work was always allied with and supported by the extremest elegance of execution. He was fond of daring experiments of color, and his pictures were a perpetual amazement and delight to artists more timid and less original, who acknowledged in the fiery young genius from Bilboa one worthy to take his place among those masters whom Paris was proud to call her own, irrespective of their birth or blood. When the war-cloud burst over France, Zamacoïs stood with his future in his grasp and the shadow of doom upon him. After the wreck was cleared, when French art numbered its dead, there was to be supplemented to those who had perished upon the field of battle the Spaniard who had become a Parisian, and who, flying before the blasts of battle, had succumbed to the mortal malady which had prevented his serving with his brethren in the ranks."

Under date of January 30, 1871, at Granada, Fortuny sends this message to Mr. W. H. Stewart: "I wish to write to you of the death of Zamacoïs, but I was so full of sorrow that my courage failed. I cannot yet believe that I shall never see him again, and it will be hard to fill his place in my remembrance." Mr. Stewart, writing to Baron Davillier, says: "I heard of Mariano Fortuny for the first time in January, 1868, through Eduardo Zamacoïs, the much lamented and talented artist, who died at Madrid January 12, 1871, at the early age of twenty-nine." It was this brilliant artist who attended Mr. Stewart on his tour to Rome, that he might, in *propria persona*, present him to Fortuny.

To symbol the art of Zamacoïs one must find an ancient Damascus blade of tempered steel with the sinister blue gleam on its edge, the hilt set with blood rubies.

WESLEY REID DAVIS.

CATALOGUE RAISONNÉ

CATALOGUE

FIRST NIGHT'S SALE

THURSDAY, FEBRUARY 3d, 1898, AT CHICKERING HALL

BEGINNING AT 8:15 O'CLOCK

BELLANGÉ

(Joseph Louis Hippolyte)

1800–1866

No. 1

Military Sketches

60 —

Pen-and-ink sketches. A squad of cavalry charging, an old man, and a group of military officers.

Signed at the right.

Height, 9 inches; length, 12 inches.

GREGORY

(Edward John)

No. 2

The War in the East

Drawing

70 —

An episode of the war in the East. The scene is dramatic, and represents a field hospital where a wounded soldier has been brought for treatment. He lies on a litter over which bends a doctor of the Red Cross service, while several comrades hold the unfortunate so that the physician can better make his diagnosis. To the right stands a soldier with a water jug.

Signed at the left.

Height, 9 inches; length, 12 inches.

PILLE

(Henri)

No. 3

Lansquenets

Pen and Ink

50 —

This is a clever drawing by the able Frenchman, in his familiar manner and of a subject he delighted to work out. It represents a parade of famous, or infamous, foot soldiers of the sixteenth or seventeenth century, marching through Paris. The abandon and the swaggering air of these rapscallions are well expressed, and to the interest of the historical fact there is the dexterous use of the medium that has made the artist famous.

Height, 13¼ inches; width, 8¼ inches.

Signed at the left. Dated 1869.

SMALL

(William)

No. 4

A Plowing Match

Drawing

125 —

An original black-and-white drawing in body color. The scene is locally English and represents a bout between farmers at the furrows. In the foreground is a plowman with a team of three horses, and on the hillside others are distributed. Groups of spectators watch the contest, and over all is a sky, gray and lowering.

Height, 14½ inches; length, 21 inches.

Signed at the right.

FORTUNY

(Mariano)

1838-1874

No. 5   310 —

Corpus Christi

A study in brown for a composition. Two figures in the center hold up a crucifix. Two drummers follow. In front the Monks carry lighted tapers. A line of buildings is behind and on a sign is displayed "Café de Las Caseras."

An interesting incident connected with the above study is mentioned in the monograph on Fortuny.

Height, 15 inches; length, 23½ inches.

Signed at the right. Dated 1869.

HARPIGNIES

(Henri)

No. 6

Autumn. Castle of San Angelo   160 —

Water Color

A dainty little landscape study by the famous master. The fall tints are happily suggested, and the remodeled mausoleum stands out in bold relief against a warm, glowing sky, with some softly suggested trees.

Height, 6¾ inches; length, 9 inches.

Signed at the left. Dated 1864.

CHAM

(Comte Amédée de Noé)

1819–1879

No. 7

The Commune

Water Color

116

Interesting sketch of some Paris characters, somewhat more serious than was usual with the famous Parisian caricaturist, so well known under the Third Empire. The two ragpickers are cleverly indicated and the color is just. Originals by this artist are rarely seen in this country.

Height, 9½ inches; width, 8 inches.

Signed at the left.

CLAYS

(Paul Jean)

No. 8

On the Coast

600

Water Color

Characteristic scene on the Holland coast. Some heavy, stolid Dutch luggers with sails of red and yellow are in the center, while to the right is a lighthouse, to the left some rowboats. Over all is a gray sky with bits of light here and there.

Height, 13¼ inches; width, 20¼ inches.

Signed at the right. Dated 1865.

MENZEL

(Adolf Frederic Erdmann)

No. 9

The Stirrup Cup

Water Color

3,375 —

A delightful and thoroughly characteristic picture by the famous German master. It portrays two horsemen in coats of mail stopping before an inn, drinking from a big cup. They are on their steeds, beneath the shadow of a large tree; and at the window of the inn, a woman and child sit looking at them. The men have all the heartiness and swashbuckle air of their time and the expression on their faces is remarkably well painted. The face of the trooper to the right of the picture is a study, being worked up to a high degree of finish, while the painting of the horses and the mail is no less able. The composition is interesting and the technique is astonishing in its detail, without the sacrifice of any of the larger qualities that go to the making of an important work.

Height, 8½ inches; length, 12 inches.

Signed at the right. Dated 1875.

FORTUNY

(Mariano)

1838-1874

No. 10

Study of Flowers

Water Color

400 —

A careful study from nature in the artist's masterly and highly searched manner. Some poppies with the long stalks and leaves, drawn on gray paper in body color.

Height, 10 inches; width, 8½ inches.

Seal at the left.

HEILBUTH

(Ferdinand)

No. 11

Monte Pincio

Water Color

The scene is laid in the famous gardens of the Pincian Hills. In the distance Rome stretches out and St. Peter's is seen vaguely in the hazy light. Two cardinals in the center of the composition are meeting on the terrace and gravely bowing to each other with courtly elegance, their servants standing in groups behind them. Although the picture is small, it is treated with great simplicity and breadth and the color scheme is one of pleasing delicacy.

Height, 7¼ inches; length, 12½ inches.

Signed at the right.

RICO

(Martin)

No. 12

Venetian Canal with View of Veronese's Tomb

A familiar view of the well-known monument, rising up behind some houses in sunlight; a bridge is to the right and a gondola and a group of trees to the left. In the right center there is a rowboat containing two men and a woman. The sky is blue with a suspicion of hazy, white clouds. Much detail is shown throughout the panel.

Height, 6½ inches; length, 11¼ inches.

Signed at the left.

ALMA-TADEMA

(Laurenz)

No. 13   3900 —

Roman Youth Reading Horace

Upon a long marble seat covered with skins and cushions, a young Roman sits reading a book. He is robed in white and purple, while the sunlight from the blue sky above him flecks the edge of his robe and sends some of its brilliancy on the stone floor, the rest of the figure and accessories being in cool shadow. There is the artist's usual skillful rendering of marble and textures, with much expression to the man's face, upon which plays a look of pleasant interest.

Height, 6¼ inches ; length, 9¼ inches.

Signed at the left. Dated 1882.

Bought by Sen W. A. Clark

RIBERA

(Roman)

No. 14

Café Chantant   3900—

A wonderfully clever piece of character painting. On the stage of a provincial concert hall a singer, dressed as a soldier, is performing his act. Beneath him are seen the orchestra and a few of the audience, each face and figure being a careful study from life. The backs of a man and a woman to the right are very expressive. A drummer, a violinist, and a flute player, are all worked up to almost photographic detail, and yet withal the panel is broadly treated.

Height, 9½ inches ; length, 12½ inches.

Signed at the right. Dated 1876.

Bought by Sen M A Clark

BOLDINI

(Giovanni)

No. 15

1050

River Seine at Mont-Valérian

A beautiful glimpse of the attractive French river under an effect of early summer, with tender greens and the sparkle of sunlight. The city stretches off to the right, some trees and a pleasure garden are to the left, and in the immediate foreground are a few boats, in one of which is a woman. Other boats dot the river here and there, and ducks are swimming about. The sky is beautifully painted, and the detail, though microscopic, is carried out broadly enough to avoid any feeling of dryness.

Height, 8¼ inches; width, 6¼ inches.

Signed at the left. Dated 1877.

FORTUNY

(Mariano)

1838-1874

2,850

No. 16

The Arquebusier

The charm of Fortuny's amazing technique is nowhere more apparent than in this famous panel of a single figure of an old soldier who stands leaning on his rest or croc with one hand, while on his shoulder is the arquebus, the quaint, clumsy gun of the middle ages. He is also armed with a big sword. The soldier is dressed in the astonishing garb of the period. He wears a doublet of green, knee breeches of red velvet, blue stockings, and a steel breast-plate, the incongruity of which is emphasized by the exquisite fidelity of the painting, a wonderful piece of realism. The man-at-arms has a head fit for strategy and crime; his rumpled hair and frowsy face betoken a dangerous foe.

Height, 9½ inches; width, 6¼ inches.

Signed at the left. Dated 1871.

MOORE

(H. Humphrey)

No. 17

Banks of a River   /25.

Mr. Moore has painted here a delightful little characteristically Japanese landscape, intensely decorative and thoroughly realistic. The branches of a graceful tree curl and twist curiously across the front and top of the picture, while on the other side of the stream which crosses the panel is the flowering bank of a beautifully cultivated garden full of delicate color, with here and there some pagodas or sculpture.

Height, 10¼ inches; width, 6¼ inches.

Signed at the left.

BONVIN

(Léon)

1834-1866

No. 18

Wild Flowers

Water Color   300

A study of growing plants and bushes, with a bit of delicate distance to the left. The careful observation and severe analysis that always characterize this artist's work are apparent here, each detail being thoughtfully worked out and drawn with exquisite fidelity.

Height, 9¼ inches; width, 7¼ inches.

Signed at the right. Dated 1864.

BONINGTON

(Richard Parkes)

1801-1828

No. 19

375 — View of Old Paris

Water Color

A delicate, colorful little drawing of the river Seine, with the old bridge of stone leading to the Cathedral of Notre Dame. The quays are shown, also the road by the stream. Paris vaguely looms up in the distance.

Height, 5½ inches; length, 8¼ inches.

Signed at the right. Dated 1827.

RICO

(Martin)

No. 20

1650 Fisherman, Seville

Water Color

A bit of river landscape, with a group of willow trees to the right, and in the center a boat in which a peasant stands fishing. On the bank beside him is a group of women and children sitting by and watching his efforts. Distant houses peep out through the trees at the back of the picture, while a blue sky flecked with white clouds is reflected in the river.

Height, 14½ inches; length, 21 inches.

Signed at the right.

BOLDINI

(Giovanni)

No. 21

The Rest at the Studio /3 6 0 —

Water Color

A characteristic composition by the dexterous Italian. The scene is the interior of a studio. A model has thrown herself down on a sofa in a pose much chosen by Boldini for his pictures. Her feet rest on a little taboret, and a white gown furnished opportunity for the skill of the artist in painting draperies. Behind the woman is an easel and behind that a piano, all properly placed, leaving the interest concentrated on the figure.

Height, 9¼ inches ; length, 13½ inches.

Signed at the left. Dated 1873.

WEBER

(Otto)

Died 1870

No. 22

Plowing 2 5 5 —

Water Color

Two sturdy white horses are dragging a plow through the earth on a hillside. Apple trees are to the left, and in the distance is seen a little valley, a barn, and an apple orchard. The sky is of late afternoon gray, with a streak of light at the horizon. The horses are drawn and painted with consummate knowledge and much skill.

Height, 10¼ inches ; length, 20¼ inches.

Signed at the right.

MESZÖLY

(Géza von)

No. 23

Farm Scene

200

On a low, flat stretch of country is seen a group of farm buildings. The farm-yard is in the foreground and a pig is seen rooting therein, while some ducks are swimming in a nearby pond. Some sunlight finds its way through a gray sky, striking the white house and the haystacks. The figure of a child is to the left center. The picture is carefully painted in much interesting detail, though not without vigor and breadth.

Height, 13¼ inches; length, 20½ inches.

Signed at the center. Dated 1882.

ZAMACOÏS

(Eduardo)

1840-1871

No. 24

Fortuny's Model

1,200

An able sketch of a woman lying, full length, on a red draped divan. She is covered with a white-and-blue drapery. A bare arm is extended along the seat; the light comes from the top and is interestingly distributed. It is a vigorous *ebauche*, deftly laid in and full of feeling.

Height, 10 inches; length, 15 inches.

Signed at the upper right.

PARSONS

(Alfred)

No. 25
English Landscape

400—

The subject is a hillside with bare trees. A general sense of autumn prevails. Through the middle of the picture runs a stream of water, and some ducks are to the left. The sky is gray, with a light streak along the horizon. The landscape forms are carefully drawn, the general anatomy of the trees being thoroughly understood and well expressed. The sobriety of the season, the general feeling of the time and place, are the result of careful observation and full appreciation of nature.

Height, 14 inches; length, 18 inches.

Signed at the right.

MADRAZO

(Raymundo de)

No. 26
Woman and Parrot

3,850—

Engrossed with portrait work in recent years, it is seldom one has a chance to see genre pictures by this able Spanish painter, so that this work comes as a revelation. It represents a luxurious interior hung with tapestry, wherein a woman dressed in yellow, with an embroidered shawl hanging loosely over her shoulders, sits playing a guitar, her feet resting on an orange-colored cushion. On a perch beside her is a white cockatoo, who strains forward to catch the ribbons on the end of her instrument. Though broadly painted throughout, there is a pleasing sense of detail, and the head and hands of the woman are carried very far as to finish, suggesting work of the careful seventeenth century Dutchmen.

Height, 19 inches; width, 15 inches.

Signed at the left.

FORTUNY

(Mariano)

1838-1874

No. 27

Arab Fantasia

A picture, one of the early *envois* sent by the artist to the Paris dealer Goupil, from Rome, and the first of his work that Mr. Stewart purchased, in which the seemingly impossible expression of terrific action has been realized. It represents a group of swarthy Arab warriors giving themselves up to a whirling, insane, howling dance. Some with long, decorative Arab guns are shooting at the earth; others are swinging similar weapons about their heads, and they are regarded with great interest by a crowd of spectators, comprising sheiks, soldiers, idlers, and others, who stand about in white and colored robes. One of the observers is mounted on his horse, the animal showing much nervousness. Fortuny has conveyed an astonishing sense of the action and wildness of the scene, faithfully reproducing the general character of the race. The picture has been called, with justice, " a veritable feat of dash of dazzling color and energetic movement."

" Zamacoïs brought me word that the dealers had an oil painting by Fortuny, and I must at once go with him to see it. We started on the instant, and found, at the Rue Chaptral, the ' Fantaisie Arabe.' My companion (Zamacoïs) went into ecstasies, calling it 'fireworks,' 'a pearl,' 'jewels,' etc., at the same time whispering to me to buy it, and not let it slip at any price."—*Reminiscences of Fortuny, by W. H. Stewart.*

Height, 20 inches; length, 26 inches.

Signed at the right. Dated 1867.

STEVENS

(Alfred)

No. 28

Alsace

1100 —

Against an open window, looking yearningly into space, a beautiful young Alsatian maiden, dressed in the picturesque costume of her province, stands musing. The light coming through the casement illumines her face and dress, and is delightfully arranged for pictorial purposes. The face has great charm, and the thoughts that are in her mind may easily be guessed. The painting is sympathetic, graceful, and full of poetic sentiment.

Height, 31¼ inches ; width, 18 inches.

Signed at the left.

MACCARI

(Cesare)

No. 29

Women at Raphael's Tomb

Water Color

700 —

The picture represents a corner of the Pantheon, in Rome, where the great Umbrian lies buried. Two women in the fashionable costume of a quarter century ago stand reading the inscription on the marble. The cleverness of the Italian school of water colorists has long been acknowledged, and the present example gives a reason therefor. The work is highly finished though kept broad, and the figures are drawn with astonishing cleverness, while all the detail is treated realistically. The marble of the pillars, the carpet on the floor, and the many little objects of minor importance that go to make up the whole are all placed with artistic judgment and dexterity. There is also a feeling of light and air throughout the edifice.

Height, 20½ inches ; width, 14¼ inches.

Signed at the right.

RICO

(Martin)

No. 30

Boats at Poissy

Water Color

A characteristic group of old canal-boats moored to the bank of the Seine, at the famous village of Poissy. The lines are picturesque and the tones of the craft are sober, with here and there a note of bright color given to the boatmen and women. To the right, on the bank, some children are playing, while in the distance a delicate line of shore is outlined in tender, hazy colors. The gray-blue sky is accented with soft white clouds.

Height, 9¼ inches; length, 13¼ inches.

Signed at the right.

FORTUNY

(Mariano)

1838–1874

No. 31

Italian Peasant Girl

Water Color

A young girl in picturesque peasant dress stands with arms akimbo beside a well. The white head-dress and waist are in striking contrast to the dark red of the skirt and the deep blue of the scarf against the stone wall. Back of her is a sky of blue, with white clouds. The drawing is delicate and true in its expression of femininity.

Height, 20¼ inches; width, 14½ inches.

Signed at the upper right. Dated 1867.

ARCOS

(Santiago)

No. 32

Buffoon

Water Color

A figure of a court jester, clad in a brilliant scarlet suit of tights and doublet, lolls asleep on a table covered with a green cloth that has partly been pushed to one side, where it hangs in big folds. One of the jester's feet is drawn up under him, the other hangs down along the edge of the table. In one of his hands, which are crossed on his lap, he holds a stick with a fool's head thereon. To the right is a large carved wood armchair, and behind the buffoon, on the wall, as a background, is a handsome piece of tapestry. The picture is highly finished, each detail being skillfully worked out, and all the surrounding still life has been carefully placed and as carefully executed.

"Arcos made studies of many figures for his painting, 'The Court of Henry III.,' among these a 'buffoon.' The model who posed for such a person one day arrived in a complete state of inebriety. Having put on his costume, he fell asleep upon a table. At that moment Mr. Stewart entered the studio—he was fond of following the work of the younger artists and encouraging them. With his usual good humor, seeing the sleeper, he exclaimed, 'He is perfect like this; make a water color of him.' The greater part of the work was painted during this seance and the model's slumber. Mr. Stewart, desiring to purchase the picture, sent M. Arcos double the price fixed."

Height, 19½ inches; width, 13½ inches.

Signed at the right. Dated 1873.

COROT

(Jean Baptiste Camille)

1796-1875

No. 33

5000 —

Ville d'Avray

A glimpse of the favorite sketching ground of the great French master. To the left is a willow tree, and behind the stream that runs across the picture there rises a hill, on which a white house catches the sunlight. In the middle of the picture is the figure of a woman. The delicate, harmonious color-sense of the famous landscapist is expressed here in his happiest manner. Mr. Stewart made a personal visit to Corot's studio in 1869 and purchased this example, since which time it has never left his possession.

Height, 11½ inches; length, 16½ inches.

Signed at the right.

TROYON

(Constant)

1810-1865

2600 —

No. 34

Valley of the Toucques

An attractive study of two cattle lying down in a field that spreads out to the distant hills in the background. A most harmonious arrangement of color gives much sentiment to the scene, and the cattle are indicated in a simple but masterly manner, characteristic of Troyon.

Height, 12½ inches; length, 17¾ inches.

Seal at the left.

DAUBIGNY

(Charles François)

1817-1878

No. 35

Auvers on the Oise

6 000 —

A stretch of smiling country under a brilliant summer sky is spread out before the spectator. To the right the river winds back to the distant hills, and is lost behind a line of trees, through which may be seen here and there the red roofs of picturesque village houses. A woman in the foreground walks toward the stream, driving some geese. The bank is full of verdure and grasses, painted in those soft, tender tones of green the artist knew so well. The landscape is drawn with consummate knowledge, with a full appreciation of the forms and subtleties of nature, while the disposition of light and shade is masterly. The master's artistic perception of beauty of line, of interesting motive, and appealing arrangement are all here.

Signed at the left. Dated 1864.

Height, 15¼ inches; length, 26¼ inches.

NITTIS

(Giuseppe de)

1846-1884

No. 36

Lowlands Near Naples

675 —

A flat stretch of water, with low-lying distance, and long graceful weeds in the foreground. A crane has started up at the right, and the sun coming through the clouds makes a blaze of light on the distant water. There is throughout a charming sense of pearly, luminous grays, while all the characteristics of marsh-land are faithfully portrayed.

Height, 9¼ inches; length, 14 inches.

Signed at the left. Dated 1873.

MADRAZO

(Raymundo de)

No. 37

Woman and Guitar

Seated in an easy chair in a garden, leaning back coquettishly, a Spanish lady is seated with a guitar. She is handsomely gowned in an evening dress of pink silk, while about her neck and shoulders is a red silk scarf. A rose-bush is to her right, and a tree to her left. The pose is graceful and natural, the woman bears the stamp of aristocratic elegance, and the painting is delicately carried out. Beautifully drawn hands, artistically painted draperies, and an agreeable, simple background of green combine to give an engaging result, and there is delightful finish everywhere, with the snap and sparkle of the brilliant school of which Madrazo is so distinguished a member.

Height, 18¼ inches; width, 14½ inches.

Signed at the right.

VAN LERIUS

(Joseph Henri François)

1823-1876

No. 38

An Old Woman's Head

A strong, vigorous portrait of an old peasant in cap and neckerchief is given with great faithfulness in a frank, personal way. The pathos of the hard life, the years of toil, and the patient suffering of poverty are all unmistakably expressed.

Height, 20½ inches; width, 15 inches.

Signed at the right. Dated 1843.

GÉRÔME

(Jean Léon)

No. 39

3,700 —

Door of a Mosque, with Heads of Decapitated Rebels

This picture represents the tragedy of a rebellion. Before a mosque at Cairo one looks through a partly opened oak door, which is elaborately ornamented, into the court. On the stone steps that lead up sits a sentinel clad in red, with his gun across his knees, a belt full of weapons, and in his hand a long pipe. He is in conversation with a janizary, who stands on guard with sword in hand and enormous pistols at his waist, costumed in a striped robe of yellow and orange, his arms, head, and shoulders protected by a mail of chain. Between them, piled up on the steps, are the heads of the Beys massacred by Salek-Kachef, all of them wonderfully realistic—pale and dripping as they have come from the necks of the offenders. Above the door hang three more ghastly trophies, a gruesome warning against rebellion. The delicate beauty of the architecture as seen through the open door, with sunlight and blue sky, serves to accentuate the somberness of the tragedy, while the careful detail and the wonderful elaboration of the artist's well-known methods have made the picture a faithful pictorial transcript of the barbaric customs of an astonishing race.

Hamerton, in speaking of the above work, says: "Gérôme governs himself so strongly as a painter that if he is immoral, it is not from irresistible impulses, but consciously and coldly. So with his love of the horrible—there is no violence, no expression of repulsion; the severed heads lie at the door at Cairo, and the sentinel smokes his pipe. A common painter would have given us bystanders with horror on their faces. But in this very coldness there is something peculiarly fascinating and terrible."

Height, 21 inches; width, 17½ inches.

Signed at the upper left.

FORTUNY

(Mariano)

1838-1874

No. 40

Arab's Head

A vigorous study, life-size, of an Arab with bared shoulders and a head-dress of white against a background of blue. The painting is a masterly sketch illustrating boldness and great rapidity of execution.

Height, 22 inches; width, 18½ inches.

Seal at the right.

ZAMACOÏS

(Eduardo)

1840-1871

No. 41

The Infanta

A portrait of the Infanta, a young Spanish princess, dressed in an elaborate gown with long train of embroidered white and blue satin. The child holds the leash of an enormous hound, while in the background is her waiting-man, half in shadow, soberly clad in gray green, wearing a wide, white linen collar, and holding in his arm a broad-brimmed hat with a scarlet feather. A look of childish fear and anticipation on the Infanta is delightfully expressed, while the dog and man serve to complete a masterly composition. The floor is of marble tiles and the background of tapestry.

Height, 23¼ inches; width, 15½ inches.

Signed at the upper left. Dated 1867.

HORSCHELT

(Theodor)

1829-1870

No. 42

An Arabian Horseman

Water Color

A rider is seated on his horse; with a shield slung over his back and gun in hand, he watches intently. Both rider and horse are painted with consummate skill and finished in great detail, being modeled carefully and with thorough knowledge. The foreground is a marsh, with long weeds and a pool of water, while in the distance a blue hill looms up. The dress is picturesque, and the trappings are brilliant in color.

Height, 16 inches; length, 18½ inches.

Signed at the right. Dated 1867.

RICO

(Martin)

No. 43

A Spanish Garden

Water Color

A Spanish garden, behind which rise the roofs of a village; the houses, with walls of white and pink tones, catch the sunlight and make brilliant notes of color. The garden is full of pots of flowers and various trees, and the treatment of the greens is solved with seeming ease. In one corner sits a man; near him is a child, while in the foreground are many ducks coming toward the spectator. Rico's command of his medium was never more apparent than in this work.

Height, 12 inches; length, 19 inches.

Signed at the left.

FORTUNY

(Mariano)

1838-1874

No. 44

3,100

Café of the Swallows

Water Color

Interior of a Moorish café. Upon a rug sits a group of Arabs, who are being served with coffee. Two columns to the right support an arch, and on a rod crossing therefrom some swallows are perched. The architectural detail in this picture is treated no less masterly than the figures in his other works, and with deft touches here and there, an idea of great detail is suggested. The result is brilliant and highly interesting, the shadows being cool and just, and giving a fine sense of perspective.

Height, 19½ inches ; width, 15½ inches.

Signed at the left. Dated 1868.

HERNANDEZ

(Don German)

No. 45

475 -

Head of a Girl

A charming rendition of young womanhood, the head and shoulders against a pink background. The dark, rippling hair is dressed with a circlet of flowers, and the eyes look roguishly out, while an exquisitely modeled hand holds a cloak of white fur from slipping away from the bare shoulders. Very freely and engagingly painted, and possessing evident spontaneity.

Height, 22 inches ; width, 18 inches.

Signed at the left.

TROYON

(Constant)

1810–1865

No. 46

Chickens Feeding

6.300 —

A Brittany woman in a white apron and cap stands feeding a flock of chickens. The row of trees in the background and some buildings are broadly indicated, while the artist has painted with great simplicity the sky and landscape, giving much attention to the fowls, which have been drawn with no little study. The picture is characteristically simple and convincingly true, being unquestionably executed before nature with great seriousness.

Height, 18½ inches ; length, 22 inches.

Signed at the left.

VAN MARCKE

(Émile)

1827–1891

No. 47

A Normandy Cow

4.150 —

This is a masterly example. The animal is seen in profile standing in a sun-lit field. The cow is brown ; has a white head, and spots on the legs. The construction and anatomy are admirable, the drawing exact, and the textures realistic. A small line of hills showing in the distance makes an interesting background.

Height, 22½ inches ; length, 33 inches.

Signed at the right.

MICHETTI

(Francesco Paolo)

No. 48
A Seaside Idyl

A charming, delicate conception. The scene represents a bit of seashore, the distant water bright with many brilliantly colored sails. In the center stand two figures amid some goats that are in advance of a herd farther back. The larger of the two figures is a young girl, partially nude, who bears across her shoulders a stick twined with leaves. Beyond her, separated by a white goat, is the figure of a nude boy who plays upon pipes. On his head is a dark hat, and about his neck is a chain. On a shore in the distance, vaguely indicated, is a group of figures. There is a feeling of cool sunshine, of balminess, and of the delight of the season, the lightness and gaiety of color keeping the canvas in a high key.

Height, 25½ inches; length, 39½ inches.

Signed at the right. Dated 1876.

BAUDRY

(Paul Jacques Aimé)

1828–1886

No. 49
Parisina

A portrait of a charming young woman in evening dress, the corsage open at the neck, with a flower placed therein. Over her shoulders is a gray wrap, and on her head is a black hat with feathers. The face is very spirituelle, and the expression one of much sweetness. The background is dark to the right and light to the left, while daintily arranged, in a decorative Arabesque line of gold, is the word "Parisina."

Height, 29 inches; width, 23½ inches.

Signed at the left.

COOSEMANS

(Joseph Théodore)

No. 50

Summer Landscape

425 —

A quiet bit of marshland is shown. The late afternoon sun catches the trees on the side of a stream, giving them a warm, golden tone. They are reflected in the quiet water, which is mirror-like in its depth and placidity. A little red-and-white house caught by the light makes a strong spot of color in the distance. A hot, simmering sky carries out the sentiment of the season and place.

Height, 18½ inches; length, 29½ inches.

Signed at the left. Dated 1868.

STEVENS

(Alfred)

No. 51

Woman and Elephant

775.-

Seated before a table which is covered with a fine Oriental rug, a woman, dressed in gray, examines the carved statuette of an elephant. Her face is exquisitely drawn, and the painting of the dress is wonderfully managed, the sense of the figure beneath being thoroughly impressed. The accessories are in the masterly manner of the great Belgian-Frenchman, while all through the work are subdued tones and harmony.

Height, 29 inches; width, 23½ inches.

Signed at the left.

FORTUNY

(Mariano)

1838-1874

No. 52

3,150

One of the "King's Moors"

Nothing could more fittingly demonstrate Fortuny's splendid mastery of his brush than this large, life-sized head of the negro Farragi (one of those called "King's Moors," who was the artist's model on his first journey in Tangiers), with brilliant contrast of the white-and-red burnous against his black skin. Both face and textures are painted in broad, vigorous strokes with thorough understanding of form and construction, and splendid appreciation of color. The white fabric with which the head and shoulders are enveloped is swept in in lines of great simplicity, every stroke being full of meaning, and the flesh painting is in the artist's best manner, large in conception and admirable in every way. To those who have only deemed the master capable of minute work this canvas will be a revelation, for he proves himself no less great in his life-size studies than in the dainty conceptions with which his name is associated.

I was speaking one day to Mr. Stewart of a fine study of a negro's head which Fortuny had in his studio in Rome, and, upon his expressing a desire to own it, I wrote to Fortuny, who sent it immediately, begging Mr. Stewart to accept it as a token of his esteem. This head is the only one of the kind the famous artist made in the same dimensions.—*Señor Raymundo de Madrazo.*

Height, 29½ inches ; width, 24 inches.

Signed at the center. Dated 1861.

FIRMAN-GIRARD

No. 53
Parisian Flower-Girl

1,600

This canvas, the first of a series of pictures of the familiar street life of the Paris flower-girl, and the one that established the artist's reputation, represents a young woman wheeling along the street a cart full of brilliantly colored roses and other growing plants. The girl, both pretty and youthful, is dressed in a striped gown with blue apron and cap. The massing of the flowers is delightfully arranged, and there are careful detail and finish everywhere.

Height, 26¾ inches ; length, 39½ inches.

Signed at the left. Dated 1872.

PINWELL

(George John)

1842-1875

No. 54
Rural Life, England
Water Color

2,150

The scene represents a lawn in front of an English country house. Two young women are reclining on the grass looking at some turkeys. At the side of them stands a lady in brown velvet, while a child in white leans on her arm. Back of them is the house ; still farther in the background are some trees and a distant view; some farm hands are to the right and left, and more turkeys are in the middle distance. The work is carried out in every detail, and the scene is characteristically English.

Height, 35½ inches ; width, 26 inches.

Signed at the left. Dated 1871.

ROTHSCHILD

(Baroness C. de)

No. 55

View of Capri

275 —

Water Color

Rising out of the water is a group of buildings. A staircase rises from the stream, and on some of the upper balconies from the walls hang many strings of red peppers. The sky is blue, with white clouds. The architecture is of the quaint Italian style that has made the place picturesque and attracted the painters.

Signed at the left.

Height, 21 inches; width, 15 inches.

FORTUNY

(Mariano)

1838-1874

No. 56

The Old Peasant

1,300 -

Water Color

A simple, sincere study of an old Italian peasant seated on the broken capital of the column of a temple. The expression of age and the heavy stolidity of the class are faithfully caught, while the treatment is in pure wash, painted directly and with the man's usual amazing command of his medium. The treatment of the head is broad, though conveying an idea of great finish, and the dress is treated in simple masses with the certainty of a master.

Height, 22 inches; width, 16 inches.

Signed at the upper right. Dated 1867.

RICO

(Martin)

No. 57

Pond at Meaux

Water Color

The tower and walls of a church form the background of the composition; here and there are tree forms that come up against the sky. In the foreground some boys sit beside a pond, which reflects the bank and the green growing on its edge. An extremely interesting variety of greens, and the arrangement is picturesque. There are also effective notes of color in the old walls of the distant buildings.

Signed at the left.

Height, 12 inches; length, 19 inches.

BOLDINI

(Giovanni)

No. 58

Clichy Square, Paris

A view of the famous square in Paris, seen under a characteristic cloud-filled sky. To the left the statue of "Marshal Moncey and the Dying Soldier" stands out, while the streets are full of action and the bustle of the French capital. The stages, drays, flower-women, and denizens of the quarter are all true to life. On the walls are the familiar signs of the different tradespeople. It is truly a glimpse of the center of the *Quartier Clichy*.

Signed at the left. Dated 1874.

Height, 21¾ inches; length, 38 inches.

COOSEMANS

(Joseph Théodore)

No. 59
Winter Landscape

This is an interesting composition, giving the view of a road vanishing off in perspective under the effect of a heavy fall of snow. To the right is a grove of trees on a high bank; to the left a hedge and a house, some other habitations stretching off in the distance. There is a fine feeling of the season, with crisp atmosphere, delightful drawing of bare trees and landscape forms. While the color is soft and harmonious, the canvas is full of rare bits of attractive painting that make it exceptionally interesting.

Height, 22 inches; length, 34 inches.

Signed at the left. Dated 1868.

MICHETTI

(Francesco Paola)

No. 60
The Turkey Girl

On a hillside, in the springtime, a young Italian girl leans against a decorative, blossoming tree, and with a face full of vague yearning looks out of the picture. Turkeys are about her; one is perched on a tree, and a large one, with outspread wings, is in the foreground. A flowering branch is near her, and all through the canvas there is a consciousness of spring that gives out a feeling of soft, balmy odors and growing vegetation. The painting is full of delicate color of a highly decorative sort, such as this artist delights in, together with a captivating cleverness of brushwork. It is Italian from the figure of the pretty girl to the deep blue of sky, the brilliancy of greens, and the pink of the blossoms.

Height, 25½ inches; length, 35½ inches.

Signed at the left. Dated 1876.

FORTUNY
(Mariano)

1838-1874

13 000

No. 61

Court of Justice, Alhambra

In a courtyard at the Alhambra, looking back into a beautiful interior, some prisoners are stretched out, their arms manacled and their feet in stocks. A dusky sentinel, clad in a white robe and red burnous, armed with warlike weapons, squats, in brilliant, shimmering sunshine, on guard over his prisoners. In the center background sits a figure on an Oriental rug, and farther in the background and shadow of the alcoves are other figures, while a distant window opens on the delicate greens of a garden. In the foreground, surrounded by a decorative tile border, is a circular fountain, filled with limpid water. To the right are some birds, and two gorgeous saddles and trappings on wooden stands. Cool shadows on the white marble contrast with the brilliant streak of sunshine, which is fairly dazzling in its intensity as it strikes the right of the picture. The drawing and painting of the intricate traceries and carvings, the hanging lamps, and the gay ornamentation of the Moorish interior are all wonderfully expressed and ably painted. As an architectural study it is delightful, for it has the truths of perspective and construction interpreted through a genuinely artistic temperament.

Height, 30 inches; width, 23½ inches.

Signed at the left. Dated 1871.

Exposition des Cent Chef d'oeuvres
Paris 1883 no 44
Bought by H Payne Whitney

HEILBUTH

(Ferdinand)

No. 62

Lady in Yellow

425

Figure of a young woman seated on a divan. She is dressed in yellow, and has a dog in her lap. About her neck is a ruff, and on her head a blue velvet hat with a white feather. The figure is charmingly posed, the light falling on one side of her head, the rest of which is in shadow. The sweet face is dignified and tender in its well-bred expression, and the painting is executed with rare grace and delicacy.

Signed at the left.

Height, 30¾ inches; width, 21¾ inches.

BONNAT

(Léon Joseph Florentin)

3,300

No. 63

Neapolitan Peasants at the Farnese Palace

This is an unusually interesting and important example of one of the rare, moderate-sized easel pictures by the distinguished Frenchman, and which was one of the successes of the Salon of 1866. A crowd of picturesque Italian country people are arranged along the stone base of one side of the palace, under a great iron-barred window. Lying fast asleep, a dark-skinned, sturdy young man in a blue cloak is stretched at full length; by his feet are a copper kettle and some clothes in a bundle. Three women in white waists and head-dresses are to the right, their faces full of expression and painted in delightful detail. To the left an old woman sleeps and a young man and girl lean against a post. On the stone pavement at their feet is a beautifully painted figure of a handsome little boy, fast asleep, his head on his arm and one hand at his face. Nothing could be more dexterously executed than the painting of this lad, clad in a jumble of garments, but with a feeling of his form beneath. The sense of youth is conveyed in every brush-mark.

Signed at the left. Dated 1865.

Height, 23¾ inches; length, 39½ inches.

VOLLON

(Antoine)

No. 64   *1700*

Crystal Bowl and Fruit

A still-life painting of a large crystal bowl standing on a table, which is draped with a red velvet cloth. There are some green and black grapes with two pears, all of which are executed with the artist's usual ease and freedom of painting, being swept in, in certain strokes, with great richness and depth.

Height, 25½ inches ; length, 36¼ inches.

Signed at the right.

ROYBET

(Ferdinand Victor Léon)

No. 65   *1,300—*

The Kitchen in the Castle

This picture depicts a scene from the middle ages wherein my lord's men of the kitchen are preparing the repast for the goodly company upstairs. Five serving-men are seen, two of whom are preparing a deer for the spit ; another is plucking a fowl and talking to a great greyhound ; still another stands over the fire, while the last is bringing in another animal on his shoulders. The work is realistically executed and full of character.

Height, 28½ inches · length, 38 inches.

Signed at the left.

DUPRAY
(Henri Louis)

No. 66
Waterloo

A French cavalry charge is depicted, the composition being filled with horsemen in excited action. In the left foreground are a number of dead English and French soldiers mingled with horses. Behind, a general on a white horse is charging forward, and beside him may be seen a detached group of combatants of both armies. The picture gives a fine idea of the horror of battle, and throughout there is much spirited movement, with fine suggestions of great masses of troops.

Height, 31½ inches ; length, 47½ inches.

Signed at the right.

DUEZ

(Ernest Ange)

No. 67

The Pont Neuf, Paris

500 — -

A glimpse of old Paris. The view is from the well-known bridge. Many important structures showing architectural detail form the background. Strongly silhouetted against an evening sky is seen the statue of Henry IV. In the foreground, along the river bank, is a line of bath-houses. A *bateau mouche* on the river and omnibuses passing over the bridge give action and interest to the composition.

Signed at the left. Dated 1884.

Height, 25¾ inches; length, 32 inches.

FORTUNY

(Mariano)

1838-1874

No. 68

Courtyard, Alhambra

2/50—

A vigorous study of old Spanish buildings and a courtyard. The walls of the buildings are strongly illuminated by the sun, and a laurel tree in blossom rises above the red-tiled roofing. In the foreground are two pigs rooting in the soft earth, while to the left of the composition are a number of chickens. Two women and a child are spreading clothes in the background. A sky of intense blue is broken by gray-white clouds.

Height, 43½ inches; width, 34½ inches.

Seal at the left.

BAUDRY

(Paul Jacques Aimé)

1828-1886

No. 69

The Wave and the Pearl

"La Vague et le Perle," by Paul Baudry, exhibited in the Salon of 1863, holds a place of honor upon the walls. Though, doubtless, its subject is familiar to many, I may briefly describe it as a nude figure of a young girl, lying with her back toward us at the edge of the ocean, and beyond her a silver-crested, emerald wave rising and shutting out the horizon completely. The girl looks as though but a moment before cast up by the waves, not dead, but living, smiling over her shoulder with a half-turned face, as though the sea was her element, and the incoming waves her breath of life. It is of no consequence from what Persian story Baudry drew this quaint conceit, if from any; the picture is its own *raison d'être*, independent of explanation and without a title. It is one of the artist's masterpieces, and in the feeling of mirthful, exuberant animal life is a reminder of some things of Correggio at Dresden. Its execution is quite brilliant. The line of the body is rhythmical, harmonious, pliable, giving to the form the effect of living, palpitating beauty.—*John C. Van Dyke, The Art Review.*

"At the time of the war this young master was in his full glory; absorbed by the work of decorating the Grand Opéra, he produced few pictures, and in spite of his desire to obtain one of his works, Mr. Stewart could not find one. Chance came to his aid and helped him well. Baudry had exhibited at the Salon of 1863 the 'La Vague et le Perle,' a picture which was the success of the year; the Empress Eugénie bought it and had it placed in her boudoir in the Tuileries, where it remained until the events of 1870. Fearing then that her personal property might be confiscated by the new government, she caused this picture and some other valuable objects to be taken to the house of a friend in the rue François Premier. The Republican Government did seize the private property of the imperial family, and a lawsuit began, which the Empress won later. Meanwhile Baudry's picture remained hidden in an attic, and it seemed that the dust might cover forever the graceful and supple form of his creation and that shining look which, as a critic says, 'pursues the spectator for a long time.'

"MM. Goupil having learned these facts, informed Mr. Stewart of them, and said he might obtain this masterpiece. After long negotiations a bargain was struck, and the picture handed over to the great collector, but on the express condition that it should be shown to no one until the trial, which was then going on, should be ended. The delivery was executed in the most mysterious manner. The transfer took place at dawn of a winter's day during a snow squall; the precious canvas, wrapped up in coarse blankets, hidden from the eyes of even those who carted it, was placed, when it reached the mansion, in the Cours la Reine, in an out-of-the-way room, the door of which for a long time opened only for friends whose discretion had been tested."

Signed at the upper left. Dated 1862.

Height, 33 inches; length, 70 inches.

SANT

(James)

No. 70   *325--*

Gipsy Fortune Teller

A composition representing a young girl incredulously listening to an old gipsy who is reading her palm. Behind the girl is her comrade, who, with her hands on her companion's shoulders, listens with a look of mingled fear and interest. Both the young women are dressed in the fashionable toilets of the day, while the old crone is in a red hood and cloak. In the background is a forest, through which the sky is gleaming. Though large and vigorously painted, the work shows careful finish and much detail of modeling, while the faces of the three figures are very expressive.

Height, 44 inches; length, 56 inches.

SECOND NIGHT'S SALE

FRIDAY, FEBRUARY 4th, 1898, AT CHICKERING HALL
BEGINNING AT 8:15 O'CLOCK

KNAUS
(Ludwig)

No. 71

The Landlord
Drawing

A truthful lead-pencil drawing of a typical German landlord, who is standing before the door of a country inn, smoking his pipe. This is a clever character study from the famous German painter, whose brush has depicted so many realistic scenes of life in the Fatherland.

Height, 18 inches; width, 12 inches.

Signed at the left.

VIÈRGE
(Daniel Vièrge Urrabieta)

No. 72

The Bridle Path, Bois de Boulogne
Drawing

A characteristic pen-and-ink sketch by the "Father of Modern Illustration." The scene represents the fashionable thoroughfare during the time of the Empire. A party of horsemen dash by, and several of the gentlemen are bowing to equestriennes approaching from an opposite direction. The certainty of touch that has made the name of Vièrge famous is all here, and the clever arrangement of composition, the introduction of innumerable figures, give a personality only found in the work of this able Spaniard.

Height, 17 inches; width, 14½ inches.

Signed at the center.

MORELLI

(Domenico)

No. 73

Woman Seated

Drawing

75.-

A drawing in pen and ink and sepia wash, representing an attractive young woman lying back in a chair. The execution is facile, and the line-work has been drawn with an easy grace and in a comprehensive manner.

It was during a trip to Naples in 1863 that Fortuny became acquainted with Morelli, a Neapolitan painter, whose work he had noticed at the exposition in Florence in 1861; he thought highly of him personally and of his talent, and was always his friend.—*Baron Davillier, Life of Fortuny.*

Signed at the right.

Height, 11¾ inches; width, 8¾ inches.

FORTUNY

(Mariano)

1838-1874

No. 74

Arab at Prayer

Monochrome

300.—

An Arab stands in devout attitude at the base of a pillar. In his belt are several pistols. The study is quite incomplete, only the feet and head, which are bare, being advanced to completion, but the drawing is most interesting as showing the artist's mode of procedure, and there may be seen therein his frankness and certainty of touch, together with his artistic conception and thorough mastery of his brush.

Height, 24 inches; width, 17 inches.

Seal at the right.

MEISSONIER

(Jean Louis Ernest)

1813-1891

No. 75

Italian Armor, Sixteenth Century

Black and White

Everything that the famous French master touched, from the simplest study to his most elaborate picture containing many figures, is not without great research and thoughtful, scholarly treatment. No subject was too insignificant for Meissonier to take pains with, for in everything he labored faithfully. The present black-and-white sketch is a study of a suit of Italian armor of the sixteenth century, which is among the treasures of the Louvre. The drawing is faultless, the detail is carefully worked out, and the result is perfect.

Height, 9 inches; width, 5¾ inches.

Signed at the right.

MEISSONIER

(Jean Louis Ernest)

1813–1891

No. 76

Armor

1250

Black and White

A study in great detail of a beautifully chased suit of French armor of the seventeenth century. The workmanship is all brought out in almost photographic minutiæ, and the sketch is characteristic of the painstaking elaboration of the master of detail and finish.

Height, 10 inches; width, 7 inches.

Signed at the right.

LAMI

(Louis Eugène)

No. 77

Off for the Hunt

Water Color

A group of men and women on horseback, in hunting costume, are seen dashing along the road, eager for the chase. Brilliant in color and with considerable movement and spirit.

Height, 5¾ inches; length, 10 inches.

Signed at the left. Dated 1864.

GAVARNI

(Guillaume Sulpice Chevalier)

1804-1866

No. 78

Small Talk

(De la tribu des Badinguet)

Water Color

A caricature of the secret police of the time of Emperor Napoleon III., nicknamed "Badinguet" ever since he was a pretender and prisoner at Fort de Ham. Two figures clad in nondescript costume are freely drawn and painted broadly in harmonious colors.

Height, 12½ inches; width, 8½ inches.

Signed at the left.

HEILBUTH

(Ferdinand)

1826-1889

No. 79

San Giovanni Laterano

500—

Water Color

A cardinal has been making a visit of state. He is just leaving, and several priests have accompanied him to his coach. Servants assist the prelate to enter. One holds the door, another takes up the trailing gown, and others group themselves about him obsequiously. Beyond is a stretch of blue hills and the white walls of the famous church. Interesting both historically and artistically.

Height, 8¼ inches; length, 14¼ inches.

Signed at the right.

FORTUNY

(Mariano)

1838-1874

2,200—

No. 80

Gipsy Caves, Granada

A study of an old thatched hovel, against the door of which are two women. The foreground is in deep shadow, while the houses are in full sunlight. There is much depth of color and powerful, vigorous painting, executed frankly, and with great simplicity.

Height, 7½ inches; width, 5¼ inches.

Signed at the left.

BENLLIURE

(José)

No. 81

House at Naples

The subject is a typical house in the poorer quarter. Around the open doorway a group of children are playing; to the left is a barrel, and to the right a chicken coop. From a window above hangs a piece of bright fabric, and flowering plants are on the window ledge.

Height, 6¼ inches; width, 4¼ inches.

Signed at the right.

BOLDINI

(Giovanni)

No. 82

The Beach at Etrétat

With his astonishing eye for the picturesque, this artist, by the natural arrangement of a few figures and boats on the pebbly beach of this French watering-place and fishing village, has made an exquisite little picture. The old fishing craft of many colors are on the shore, and are indicated broadly yet with microscopic finish; the sails, spars, ropes, and impedimenta being painted in minute detail. In front, and to the right, a fish-wife, whose dress has been caught by the wind, is walking along the beach, carrying a child, while immediately in the foreground a little boy is lying at full length on the pebbles. The sea, which is of deep blue, is swept with wind clouds.

Height, 5¼ inches; length, 9¼ inches.

Signed at the right.

PETTENKOFEN

(Auguste von)

No. 83

425.00

A Market in Hungary

The scene represents a country market. Near an old building is assembled a number of peasants, who are seated about on the ground and on benches. To the left are some horses and wagons. All is very broadly painted in agreeable colors and with great care as to details, the artist being known as the "Austrian Meissonier."

Height, 5½ inches; length, 9 inches.

Signed at the right.

Sold in Mathiesen Sale 1902 600.00

RICO

(Martin)

No. 84

The Tarpeian Rock, Rome

$2,000$ -

A series of terraces of the cliff of the Capitoline Hill, crowned by a building of pink stucco, all in bright sunlight, under a blue sky flecked with white clouds. A cart drawn by two donkeys, some hucksters, and a little dog are seen in the foreground, while at the lower edge of the composition are a flight of steps and a stone post. Though the panel is small, every detail is carried out faithfully, and the treatment is a marvel of dexterous technique.

Height, 6½ inches; length, 11 inches.

Signed at the left.

FORTUNY

(Mariano)

1838–1874

No. 85

Breakfast in the Old Convent Yard

This modest little panel is an extraordinary example of detail painting and displays the remarkable facility of the great Spaniard. The scene represents a courtyard of an old convent; the walls of the building, made a radiant white by the sunshine, form an interesting background. The tiled roof of the ancient edifice throws cool, bluish shadows, as does a daintily suggested grapevine to the left. Behind, and seen above the wall, is a dense grove of orange trees, while a warm summer sky is broken with white clouds. A group of cavaliers, who have halted on their journey, are seated at a table breakfasting, and, although of minute proportion, are painted with exquisite detail as to costume and all accessories. The expression of satisfaction, the postures, and the general arrangement of the four men are all wonderfully realized. Some chickens about the table peck at the crumbs, while by a distant door a serving-man talks to a peasant, near whom are two sedan chairs, evidently belonging to a lady who leans pensively on the balcony, gazing at the cavaliers seated at the table. A number of large water jars are ranged along the right side of the picture, against the shadow of a building, from which hangs a lamp.

Height, 10½ inches; length, 13½ inches.

Signed at the left.

ZAMACOÏS

(Eduardo)

1840–1871

No. 86

The Snowball   1,200 -

In a pathway of a woods are two men dressed in brilliant colored costumes of the middle ages. They have thrown a snowball, which a dog is chasing in full cry. There is an effect of evening light on the snow; the animal is full of expression and painted with the wonderful detail so characteristic of the brilliant young genius, whose untimely death at twenty-nine was so distinct a loss to the cause of art.

Height, 7½ inches; width, 5¼ inches.

Signed at the left. Dated 1868.

RICO

(Martin)

No. 87

The Woodcutter   400 -

Water Color

A summer landscape, painted in the village of Meaux, France. In the foreground are a woodchopper, a wheelbarrow, and a group of children; while behind him, to the middle of the composition, rise two poplar trees. To the right and left, groups of houses are discernible, while over all is a brilliant, flecky sky, with soft white clouds. The greens are skilfully managed in a variety of tones, running from the brilliant color of the trees in the immediate foreground to the tender tones in the distance, the whole being treated in pure wash and very simply.

Height, 14½ inches; width, 21 inches.

WEBER

(Otto)

Died 1870

No. 88

Landscape and Cows

Water Color

500

A pastoral scene, with cattle and distant blue hills. At the right center are some trees and a stone wall. The cows are well drawn and modeled, and the foreground is painted with much fidelity and care. A gray-blue sky lends interest to the composition, which, as a whole, is most satisfactory.

Height, 12½ inches ; length, 20 inches.

Signed at the left.

PETTENKOFEN

(Auguste von)

No. 89

2.500 —

Hungarian Peasant Wagon

The admirable methods of this able painter are seen to great advantage in this small, though broadly executed picture of two donkeys harnessed to a peasant's cart, in which are seated two children. The place is a field, with stacks of grain and heaps of pumpkins. The time is nearly midday, and the strong light from a cloudless blue sky gives a wealth of warm color to the scene.

Height, 10½ inches ; length, 15½ inches.

Signed at the right. Dated 1878.

BOLDINI

(Giovanni)

No. 90   *1250.*

Pond in the Forest of Fontainebleau

This is an unusual vista of the famous wood, but no less true than those of more familiar aspect. Instead of the heavy, sturdy oaks generally painted, there are some white birches and delicate, graceful tree-forms, with light bits of green and trailing branches. Bare rocks show here and there, contrasting with the darker greens of the undergrowth, and in the foreground, among the long sedge grasses, a woman is filling a bucket with water. The distance is tender and the sky filled with beautifully modeled cloud-forms. It is unnecessary to add that no detail has been spared that could make the composition complete, and throughout there is an amazing sense of the brilliancy of light and air.

Height, 11 inches; length, 19¼ inches.

Signed at the left.

FORTUNY

(Mariano)

1838–1874

No. 91

Rosa Contadina   *1100 —*

Water Color

An Italian girl leans against a wall. Her head drops on her breast, and in her hand she holds some roses. The head is finished in great detail, and the rest of the figure is painted with much freedom. The wall behind her is very delicate in color, being almost white. This is a characteristic example of the master.

Height, 17½ inches; width, 10½ inches.

Signed at the upper right. Dated 1867.

RICO

(Martin)

No. 92

Seville

1350

Water Color

M. Rico has caught the sentiment and sparkle of the light and brilliancy of Spanish sunlight, and treated this picture with much freedom and dash. The scene represents a garden, with the town in the distance. To the right is a house, with a wall of faded red that glows warm and bright in the sunlight, and in front of it is a leafless tree, the drawing and painting of which are most clever, showing wonderful command of the medium. In the middle of the composition two donkeys stand, and from the gate a woman is seen coming out. She wears a bright red shawl, that adds the necessary note of color.

Height, 12 inches ; length, 19 inches.

Signed at the left.

STEVENS

(Alfred)

No. 93

1600

Remembrance and Regrets

This composition of a single figure is very characteristic of the artist's well-known manner. It represents a beautiful *Parisienne du Haute Monde*, exquisitely gowned in white. She sits on an easy chair, resting her head on one hand, and holding a letter in the other. Beside her, on a dressing table, a mirror reflects her head. On the left some wraps and a parasol are carelessly placed. The face, full of thoughtful tenderness, is troubled, and at a glance one may read the story as conveyed in the title.

Height, 24 inches ; width, 18 inches.

Signed at the left.

FORTUNY
(Mariano)
1838-1874

No. 94   4/00 —

Arab Reclining on a Divan
Water Color

A richly dressed Arab, with a sword in his girdle, half seated and half lying on a divan. Beside him is a taboret with a cafetière and cup. A gun-rack with richly ornamented weapons occupies the wall. The figure and accessories are painted with a brisk and accurate touch and with great fidelity to detail, while the surroundings are washed in with great breadth and vigor of effect.

Height, 27¼ inches ; width, 18½ inches.

Signed at the right. Dated 1869.

RIBERA
(Roman)

No. 95   2 (150 —

Café Ambulant

This is a fine study of a characteristic street scene somewhere in the Latin quarter of Paris. All the actors of the little comedy are there in unconscious attitude, preoccupied each with his own affairs. The shabby patrons of the perambulatory coffee-stand, the jaunty, careless art students, the gaping tinker's boy, the gossiping women, and the busy cobbler in his bric-à-brac stall, are all treated with great fidelity and a rare quality of observation, enriched by a keen sense of humor. While the artist has paid the strictest attention to detail, and has painted every object with wonderful accuracy, he has preserved a delicacy of atmospheric effect, a charm of color, and a distinction of tone which command the highest admiration.

Height, 19¼ inches ; length, 34¼ inches.

Signed at the right. Dated 1878.

MICHETTI

(Francesco Paolo)

No. 96

Spring

In a bright summer landscape, on a hillside crowned with a large stone building and covered with a growth of underbrush and trees, lies a cabbage garden. A pretty girl tending a flock of turkeys has been met on her way home by an ardent swain, who, with rustic fervor, tries to steal a kiss. The figures are executed with a facile and accurate touch, the turkeys are painted with great cleverness, and the tender green tones of the cabbages, so difficult to portray properly, are admirably realized. All the vigor and fertile invention of this skillful Italian painter are accentuated in this picture.

Height, 20½ inches; length, 33 inches.

Signed at the left. Dated 1876.

DECAMPS

(Alexandre Gabriel)

1817–1878

No. 97

Death and the Woodman

The subject is chosen from the well-known fable of La Fontaine. On a rock in a forest, at sunset, sits white-robed Death, and beside him the woodman, wretched and poverty-stricken, in an attitude of supreme dejection. He has asked the grim specter to relieve him of his troubles, and, now the dread terror is so near at hand, he is overcome with fear and filled with a desire to live.

Height, 28 inches; width, 23 inches.

Signed at the right.

COROT

(Jean Baptiste Camille)

1796-1875

No. 98

6,200—

Sunset

A pleasant glade in early summer twilight. To the right, young trees stand out a little from the forest. At the foot of two trees, at the left, are two women, one of whom is nude and is seen in shadow; both figures are merely notes in the landscape. A soft, silvery distance stretches away in the middle of the picture, and a sky full of luminosity is made brilliant by the setting sun. There is a fine sense of enveloping atmosphere in this little masterpiece, an example in which Corot is seen in his most poetic mood.

Height, 23 inches; width, 16½ inches.

Signed at the left.

ROUSSEAU

(Théodore)

1812-1867

No. 99

7,450

The Woodcutter, Forest of Fontainebleau

A glade in the forest of Fontainebleau, in the clearing of which a woodcutter piles up some wood. In the middle distance is a pond, beyond which, on high ground, is a group of buildings, and to the left is a group of fine old trees rich in autumnal colors and the warm glow of the late afternoon sun. The tree-forms are carried out with conscientious care and with rare analytic power, while the drawing of the branches and tree-trunks is no less accurate and masterly. There is a fine feeling of atmosphere throughout the work, great distance, and a feeling of the season of the year.

Height, 25½ inches; width, 21¼ inches.

Signed at the left.

TROYON

(Constant)

1810–1865

No. 100

13.700 —   The Lane

A summer landscape, showing the turn of a lane in the woods; the sunlight gleaming through the trees and lighting the ground here and there. A man and child are seen coming down a decline at the left, and to the right, just beyond the turn of the lane, is a woman with a basket on her arm. There is a sense of depth and sobriety to the greens, with beautiful tree drawing and construction, and a feeling of the solemn stillness and attractive loneliness of the woods is poetically and engagingly expressed.

Height, 23 inches; width, 19 inches.

Signed at the left.

ZAMACOÏS

(Eduardo)

1840–1871

No. 101

10.700 —   Checkmated

Two shrewd little hunchbacks in quaint costumes sit on a table. One, his face bright with mischief and wit, has been playing a game of chess with a jester, who sits facing him and whom he has just checkmated. The court jester is clad in brilliant scarlet, with cap and bells, and he leans in contemplative mood, resting his chin on his hand. The background is a fine piece of tapestry, and the table is covered with a sumptuous Oriental rug. A handsome leather chair is to the right; on this is a fool's baton, while a glove lies on the floor. The light, which falls on the figures, produces a striking effect.

Signed at the right. Dated 1867.

Height, 19¾ inches; length, 24 inches.

FORTUNY
(Mariano)

1838-1874

No. 102

The Masquerade

4750 -

Water Color

An important and characteristic composition, showing the great facility of the artist and his originality of invention. The scene is laid in the garden of the Tuileries. On a stone seat a Harlequin stands scraping his kit, and in front of him is a group of two masked women and two men, one of whom is a Moor, in gorgeous robes and turban, and the other, in wig and knee breeches, leans jauntily on a long cane. To the right two men lean over a marble balustrade. In the distance many maskers are dancing. There are great brilliancy of sunlight and a sparkle of color throughout, and the important center group is worked out in much detail.

Height, 17½ inches ; length, 24½ inches.

Signed at the right. Dated 1868.

BAUDRY
(Paul Jacques Aimé)

1828-1886

No. 103

Fortune and the Child

6500 -

This picture, which is a reduction of the famous painting in the Luxembourg, Paris, represents two figures, a woman and a child, seated on the side of a fountain. Both are nude, though under and behind them are some draperies. A landscape stretches out in the background, and a group of trees are to the right. The wheel of fortune, with chain and padlock, lies at the woman's feet. The flesh tones are exquisite, and the face of the woman is of idyllic beauty, painted with consummate ability and tenderness.

Height, 32¾ inches ; width, 23½ inches.

Signed at the right. Dated 1853.

BOLDINI

(Giovanni)

No. 104

2.275

River Seine, at Bougival

A beautiful glimpse of the river at the quaint little town near Paris, taken at its most attractive season. The stream passes through charming country and beside a fine old formal garden, with square-cut box hedge and handsome stone gates. The foliage indicates early summer, with dainty, sparkling greens and long tangle of rushes in the foreground. The shadows are reflected in the water, and in the middle of the river is a punt in which are a man and two women. The figures are delicately suggested, and give the touch of needed color. The sky is blue, with a few white clouds, and the painting is fascinating in its wonderfully dexterous handling.

Height, 21½ inches; width, 16 inches.

Signed at the left. Dated 1874.

CLAYS

(Paul Jean)

No. 105

1900 —

Dead Calm

A motive, in which this admirable painter is thoroughly at home, represents a perfectly quiet river, with the low, flat Holland land in the distance, and here and there the characteristic red-tiled roofs. Three big sailing vessels lie listlessly drifting; their sails, now and then caught by sunlight, are flapping idly and are reflected in the water. A ship's boat is pulling off from one of the bigger crafts. An old buoy to the left is motionless, and against the shore and rocks to the right the water barely ripples.

Height, 25½ inches; length, 43½ inches.

Signed at the right. Dated 1868.

FORTUNY

(Mariano)

1838–1874

No. 106

A Street in Tangiers

Water Color

A group of Arabs lazily reclining under the shadow of a wall in a dingy street. To the right is a vista of another street, that goes off at right angles through archways enlivened now and then by full sunlight. A horse stands to the extreme left of the picture, and beside him two Arabs are talking. Above is a window with tracery of carved woodwork. A figure in the foreground, for which Henri Regnault served as model, stands with bared shoulders, giving the artist a chance to show his able treatment and modeling of flesh. The bare feet and legs of another Oriental lying down, further demonstrates M. Fortuny's dexterity with the brush. The story of Mr. Stewart's acquisition of this picture is interesting. Fortuny had heard a great deal about the great French painter Meissonier, but had never seen his work except through photographic reproductions. Mr. Stewart knowing this, wished to cause a pleasure to his new friend, as a propitiatory present. He took to Rome the little masterpiece of Meissonier which is in this collection, "The End of a Game of Cards," and Fortuny, to his surprise, found one morning the great master's panel placed on his own easel and lighting up his studio. Deeply touched, the artist wrote a few words of dedication under the water color, "A Street in Tangiers," and presented it to Mr. Stewart.

Height, 14¼ inches; length, 19¾ inches.

Signed at the right. Dated 1869.

NITTIS

(Giuseppe de)

1846-1884

No. 107

Route from Brindisi to Barletta

The picture is one of a long road leading over a bridge, along which some weary-looking pedestrians, with a team and yellow-bodied wagon, are slowly moving. The fine dust seems a foot deep in the highway, the bushes and grass are covered with it, the sunlight is blazing, and the heat, like the breath of a blast-furnace, is rising up in wavy lines from the earth. The idea of sultriness is overpowering. We almost feel it, as we do in reading the opening chapter of "Little Dorrit," with its description of Marseilles burning in the sun. To convey this impression, this feeling, seems to have been the one object of the artist, and he has succeeded in doing it. It is faint praise to say that the picture is well painted, for it is more than that. The color-scheme is light, not fiery; the composition and perspective are excellent, and the textures, from the powdered dust and the wilted herbage to the iron tires of the wagon-wheels and the clothes of the travelers, are painted with a directness and a certainty not always visible in De Nittis's pictures of the Champs Elysées.—*John C. Van Dyke, The Art Review.*

Signed at the right. Dated 1872.

Height, 11¼ inches; length, 21¼ inches.

RICO

(Martin)

No. 108

Plaza and Street, Toledo

3,050

Prominently in the middle background, to the right of the composition, is a great white stuccoed building, with an elaborate wooden door studded with iron ornaments and topped with a carved coping, over which are two griffins. Birdcages hang on the wall, and a window protected by an iron grille is filled with flower-pots containing trailing vines. A child in a yellow dress stands in the shadow, and two donkeys browse lazily, a little dog lying near them. The foreground is most delicately suggested, while to the extreme right a street recedes in the distance. The sky is a heavy blue, and the atmosphere is hot and simmering.

Signed at the right.

Height, 8¼ inches; length, 13¼ inches

RICO

(Martin)

No. 109

Avenue Josephine Market, Paris

2,500

A glimpse of one of the Paris out-of-door markets. Across the middle of the panel is a line of green-colored booths or sheds, against which are banked carts, and groups of market people and buyers are trading. In the background is a vista of Paris, and in the foreground are great numbers of jugs and pots, evidently the wares of a pottery merchant. Though there is apparently an enormous amount of detail in the picture, it is more by reason of the astonishing cleverness of suggestion than in any labored work. This painting was first shown at the Universal Exposition of 1878.

Height, 6⅝ inches; length, 11¼ inches.

Signed at the right.

MEISSONIER

(Jean Louis Ernest)

1813–1891

No. 110

The End of a Game of Cards

A tragedy admirably told on the few inches of a small panel by one of the masters of this century. Two cavaliers have had some quarrel about a doubtful throw; they have drawn their swords and pursued each other across the room, upsetting and breaking the furniture. One is now stretched on the ground near the reddened blade which defended him; the other, struck to death, too, is dying at the back of the room, trying to stop with weakened hand the flow of blood from his pierced breast. Meanwhile the table on which they cast the dice or cut the cards, upset during the fight, burns smouldering in the fireplace. The fatal passion has annihilated all, both the actors in the drama and the scene of the struggle. The conception is that of a thinker; the picture, painted with wonderful understanding of chiaroscuro, is executed with that precision without affectation, that firmness without dryness, that breadth of touch which make the little compositions of the master so great.

Height, 8¾ inches; width, 7¼ inches.

Signed at the right. Dated 1865.

FORTUNY

(Mariano)

1838–1874

No. 111

Meissonier's Portrait

2,300

A clever sketch of the great painter of "La Rixe." He stands in one corner of his own studio, at Poissy, dressed in top-boots, tight white breeches, and a brown velvet coat. His head is in profile, and in his left hand he holds an enormous cavalry sabre. The legs in particular are carefully painted, the rest being nevertheless highly suggestive. Meissonier, it seems, had called on Fortuny one day while the latter was painting his "Spanish Marriage," and had criticised one of the soldiers in that canvas, asserting that, for a good cavalry officer, his legs were not in proportion to his body, and to support his assertion and persuade the young man, who was more astonished than convinced, he drew his attention to his own legs, which were in perfect proportion, and said, "I am the only man who has the proper legs for the character you need, and if you will come out to Poissy I will serve as your model." Fortuny accepted, went to Poissy, and made a sketch of the great master, who was much astonished at the rapidity of execution. Completed later, this study became the "Portrait of Meissonier," the artist reproducing the famous painter's studio as a background, including an easel on which is the sketch for a composition called "Le Guide."

Height, 11 inches; width, 6½ inches.

Seal at the right.

MEISSONIER

(Jean Louis Ernest)

1813-1891

No. 112

The Stirrup Cup

A subject of which the artist was fond and which he has treated several times. It is always the gentleman on horseback quenching his thirst before he gallops off. Here Meissonier triumphs through the truth of the attitudes, the simplicity, and the naturalness of the motions, the happy rendering of the expression of the faces; here is shown with rare intensity the great knowledge of the master with regard to everything that concerned the horse. Meissonier loved the horse passionately; he modeled some in wax, which are little masterpieces that Barye would have been glad to sign. "He knew not only the structure and the appearance of the noble animal, but he had caught its nature, guessed its caprices and revolts. His horses, wherever you find them in his works, have not only their breed, but their character, well marked. In this picture the horse, a portrait of an animal that he knew and loved, is a marvel of life and of perfect modeling.

Height, 6½ inches; width, 4½ inches.

Signed at the left. Dated 1864.

RICO

(Martin)

No. 113

Rienzi's House in Rome

A view of the ancient building, the supporting pillars of which are half walled up. To the left, in sunlight and shadow, a street is seen, and a number of beggars are grouped about on a grassy foreground to the left. There is a deep blue sky, with brilliant white clouds.

Height, 6 inches; length, 11 inches.

Signed at the left.

FORTUNY

(Mariano)

1838–1874

No. 114   42,000

The Choice of a Model

In an elaborately decorated and sumptuously furnished apartment of the Palazzo Colonna, in Rome, a number of members of the Academy of Saint Luke, at the most luxurious period of last century, are assembled to criticize a nude female model who is posing before them in an attitude of studied grace. The ultra-fashionable costumes of the men and their pompous and artificial manners, no less than the wonderful richness and elegance of their surroundings, indicate to what an extent the study of art was at this period indulged in as a fashionable accomplishment. The subject has given Fortuny the best possible opportunity for the exercise of his unique skill in the treatment of rich draperies, fine metal work, choice marbles, and all the glitter and splendor of precious objects of art with which the princely apartment is filled to overflowing. Nor has the artist been too much preoccupied with the imitation of textiles and with the difficult problems of intricate design and arrangement, for he has treated with characteristic skill the delicate contrasts of tone and color as well as the differences of human type and expression, which alone would distinguish the picture as a rare artistic accomplishment. With all the extraordinary elaboration of detail and amazing wealth of color the general harmony of the picture is maintained without a false note, and it will always rank as the highest expression of Fortuny's great inventive power, his rare taste, and his consummate facility of execution.

Height, 21 inches ; length, 32 inches.

Signed at the right. Dated 1874.

BOLDINI

(Giovanni)

No. 115

Highway of Combes-la-Ville

Along a white, flat road, with the distant view of a small village of white walls and red roofs, a few wagons are seen going and coming, while on a side path people are slowly walking along under a row of long, slender trees. To the right is a gray stucco wall, showing the red brick at the entrance gates, where several women stand talking. To the left is a stretch of slightly undulating country, and above is a sky filled with brilliant cloud-forms. Nowhere has the artist evolved more dexterity or more feeling for the realization of the sparkle of a burning summer day in France. The strong light of the sun and the great intensity of the heat are masterly rendered, and the tenderness and brilliancy of the greens are truthfully conveyed. It required all the skill of the painter's hand, all the science that his eye possessed, to dare to undertake such a work. It has taken all his talent to make it successful. The subject was one of those which in art they call dangerous; almost in play he has overcome immense difficulties.

Height, 27 inches; length, 39½ inches.

Signed at the left. Dated 1873.

FORTUNY
(Mariano)
1838–1874

No. 116
Dead Girl

800

When Fortuny was at Granada, a daughter of one of the attendants in the Alhambra died. The father came to the artist and begged him to make a painting of his daughter, that he might have some likeness of her. So Fortuny painted her lying dead in her coffin—painted her as only such a subject could be painted, broadly, boldly, swiftly—and in every brush-stroke of it there is that feeling of power that we experience in viewing the drawings of Michel Angelo. In the most delicate as in the broadest sweep of the brush there is the sense of strength. The spirit of death—I had almost said death itself—is caught and transfixed upon canvas by a master hand that would rather have left it undone, but, having it to do, did it swiftly and surely. One must be more than simply "clever" to do such work. One must look deep into the essence of things—and that is genius.—*John C. Van Dyke, The Art Review.*

Height, 22½ inches; length, 27½ inches.

Signed at the left.

TROYON
(Constant)
1810–1865

No. 117
Cow Among the Cabbages

12,000—

In a cabbage patch, against a well-composed sky, stands a white cow, marked with red on the face and neck. To the right are some willow trees, and vaguely seen in the distance is a stretch of flat country, with hills along the horizon. It is one of the sober, thoughtful studies of cows that none knew how to execute so well as this master. The characteristics of the beast, the drawing and anatomy, the relations of light and shade, and the proper appreciation of form and movement make this work a masterpiece.

Height, 36 inches; width, 29 inches.

Signed at the left.

LEIBL

(Wilhelm)

No. 118
Village Politicians

15,000

A most important canvas by this great German master. A group of four old peasants sit attentively listening to a younger man, who is reading from a newspaper. Each particular face and figure is a study by itself, Holbeinesque in its marvelous search for character and extraordinary finish. So masterly is the treatment, that none of the types of character illustrated are unduly assertive, and all contribute to make a splendid harmony. The artist has accentuated the difficulties of his task by introducing no less than four pairs of hands, yet these he has drawn and painted no less freely and skillfully than the faces, the picture, in its wonderful fidelity and ability, being reminiscent of the Dutch masters of the seventeenth century. It is the master-work of Leibl, and as such created a sensation in Paris at the Universal Exposition of 1878.

Height, 31 inches ; length, 39 inches.

FORTUNY

(Mariano)

1838-1874

No. 119   *15,200—*

The Antiquary

In a room littered with biblios, bric-à-brac, and articles of virtu an enthusiastic amateur sits with a portfolio on his lap, admiring a rare engraving. In front of him, on a carved chair, is a folio of prints. Behind the antiquary, a friend leans over his chair and glances at the engraving which is being admired by the amateur. On a rich rug that nearly covers the floor is an elaborately carved treasure chest, on which are placed specimens of Venetian glass and other objects; a handsome large red vase stands on the mantle, and a cockatoo is perched on a bar in the foreground, while at the extreme right a man carrying a portfolio stops in front of an elaborately carved table. A suit of Japanese armor stands near the left center, and the walls of the room are hung with rich tapestries. In a gorgeous Florentine frame, hanging above a carved white marble fireplace, is a painting of a knight in armor, a likeness of Mr. Stewart, which was introduced under the following circumstances. Mr. Stewart had been in possession of this work for some time when Fortuny made a trip to Paris, and while there called on his patron. In chatting with him, Mrs. Stewart expressed her regret at not having a good portrait of her husband. Fortuny did not answer, but a little later he went up to "The Antiquary," and, with a certain appearance of embarrassment, declared that the background needed retouching. An artist's fancy, they thought. Mr. Stewart was one of those men who refused nothing, and Fortuny was one of those to whom everything was granted, and on his departure he carried away the picture. After a few days, when it was returned to the owner, it had in fact been subjected to a change. The artist had introduced in the background a capital portrait of his friend, which, in its old frame, thoroughly harmonized with the original composition of the picture.

Height, 19 inches; length, 26 inches.

Signed at the right.

MADRAZO

(Raymundo de)

No. 120

Departure from the Masked Ball

This well-known canvas represents the courtyard of a Parisian mansion at the conclusion of a masked ball. It is early dawn, and the gas-lamps at the gates seem feeble in the greater light of the day that is so near. Carriages, in which are gay maskers in costume, are being driven away, and other guests are coming down the canopy-covered steps of the mansion. A group of footmen and coachmen in livery are at the left, discussing the contents of a daily paper. In the middle group a man dressed as Punchinello, with a Japanese lady on his arm, is taking a Madame de Pompadour to task. Beyond, a Pierrot, somewhat the worse for his dissipation, has dropped on the grass, and his companion is assisting him to rise. Outside, some street-sweepers, half awake, are cleaning up the road—a dramatic touch. Leafless trees, beautifully drawn, are in front of the handsome iron railings which inclose the courtyard, and the distant houses are pale and gray in the early morning light. No detail has been omitted, everything is in harmony, and the composition is most interestingly arranged. This picture attracted great attention when it was shown at the Salon, 1878, and marks the highest point in the *genre* work of this distinguished painter's career.

Height, 27½ inches; length, 46 inches.

Signed at the left.

FORTUNY
(Mariano)

No. 121
Arab Butcher

2.300

A ray of glaring sunlight falling on a white wall, a slaughtered ox stretched upon the ground in a pool of blood, a figure or two with just enough color in the costumes to make contrast — and that is all. Repulsive as the subject undoubtedly is, one can but wonder at the genius of the man which could transform such a scene into a thing of beauty. And it is actually beautiful from an artist's point of view. The heated air, the glaring sunlight, and, above all, the key of color formed by the bright red blood, are startling in their effectiveness and are really pleasing to the eye. Nor is the sketch idealized in the popular meaning of that badly abused word. It is natural enough, yet it is not simply a piece of brutal strength, like Rembrandt's "Dressed Beef" in the Louvre.—*John C. Van Dyke, The Art Review.*

I have in view several other things, one especially ("The Butcher") that I will endeavor to sketch before my departure, but it will not be for sale, for nobody would buy it, only I will take the luxury of painting it for myself; it is in this that true painting consists.—*Extract from Fortuny's letter to Baron Davillier, October 9, 1874.*

Seal at the left.

Height, 39 inches; length, 52 inches.

VAN MARCKE
(Émile)

No. 122
Cows in the Valley, Toucques

11.500

A complete and fine example of the well-known cattle-painter, who has here composed an agreeable arrangement of animals and a summer landscape. A white cow in profile is in the foreground, half in sunlight; behind her is a black one, while to the left a red cow is lying down near a pool of water. Other cattle are vaguely seen in the distance, also a plain and a hillside in tender purples. A white building is nearly obscured by some trees, and there is a sense of the rich, heavy summer greens, cool shadows, and the quiet of pasture lands.

Signed at the left.

Height, 24 inches; length, 40 inches.

STEWART

(Julius L.)

No. 123

Summer

1,000

The scene represents a field of grain situated in a hollow surrounded by verdure-clad hills, soft and harmonious in their tender purples and green, under a sparkling sky of cerulean blue, with fluffy white clouds. To the right is a tree almost leafless, and near it are two fashionably dressed women, one in white, the other in gray. To the left center are a man and woman, with red parasol, while near by is a young lad. The red tones of poppies, scattered here and there among the grain, give note of color, while the greens both in the foreground and middle distance are pure, brilliant, and admirably arranged. A cloud shadow falling on the field serves to make pleasing contrasts of light and shade, and the painting, though broad and vigorous, is not without much detail. Above all, the work has a crisp, fresh, breezy feeling, suggesting satisfactorily the time—early summer—and the place—France.

Signed to the right. Dated 1880.

Height, 33½ inches; length, 59 inches.

FORTUNY

(Mariano)

No. 124

Environs de Tanger

1,400

An *ébauche*, or the laying-in of a picture. An old, uprooted tree is to the left, and to the right are suggestions of figures about a hut. In the distance, to one side, is a stream of water, and in the middle the ruins of a square, low building. The work is painted in free, vigorous strokes, each one of which is full of significance, and demonstrates the artist's manner of approaching an important composition, and as such is most interesting.

Height, 26½ inches; length, 40 inches.

Seal at the left.

VOLLON

(Antoine)

No. 125

Monkey and Fruit

2,100

This large and highly characteristic example of the great modern master of still-life painting represents a table covered with various articles in great confusion, the result of the caprice and mischievousness of a monkey, who is looking from the dim background at the havoc he has wrought. With one paw he is toppling over a copper vase of flowers, and with the other a glass dish, the fruit from which is strewn on a large plate. A big red book, a pipe, and some sheets of music are scattered about.

Height, 59 inches; length, 43 inches.

In Layton Art Gallery Milwaukee

ROMAKO

(Anton)

No. 126

The Huntress

375

Portrait of a woman in deep-red doublet, white ruff about the neck, and wearing a large hat with feathers, and carrying on her shoulder an old arquebus. The face has a piquant expression, and is painted with great freedom and dash.

Height, 36 inches; width, 26½ inches.

Signed at the right.

FORTUNY

(Mariano)

No. 127

7000 — The Alberca Court, Alhambra

An incomplete but marvelously composed interior of the famous court, with the basin of the fountain in the foreground, the limpid water reflecting the exquisite Moorish architecture and the long graceful columns. An entrance opens into another court, and farther on is seen, vaguely, a garden. To the right are some plants with great leaves and an orange tree. An elaborate Oriental rug hangs from the roof, and a curtain protects the left of the court from the heat of the sun. The possibilities of the picture seem infinite, and in its unfinished state it gives an interesting idea of the artist's manner of procedure.

Height, 48 inches ; length, 67 inches.

Seal at the right.

MADRAZO

(Raymundo de)

No. 128

5000 — Pierrette

A full-length figure of a pretty girl in fancy dress, as Pierrette, leaning against a wall and holding a black mask in one hand. A pink cloak jauntily thrown over her shoulders, relieved by a blue lining and ermine border ; a pink sash and stockings, a white petticoat and slippers, make a costume as tasteful in arrangement as it is piquant in effect. The painting is executed with a freedom and spirit quite in harmony with the subject, and the picture has enjoyed great popularity even in the reproduction by which it is best known.

Height, 78½ inches ; width, 37 inches.

Signed at the upper right.

BRONZES, FURNITURE, AND OTHER OBJECTS

BRONZES, FURNITURE, ETC.

TO BE SOLD AT CHICKERING HALL, FRIDAY NIGHT, FEBRUARY 4th

AT THE CONCLUSION OF THE SALE OF PAINTINGS

No. 129
STATUETTE IN BRONZE

65—

"The Communist," by d'Épinay. Golden-brown patina.

Signed and inscribed.

Height, 16 inches.

No. 130
PAIR JAPANESE BRONZE VASES

20—

By Shō-kwa-ken. Straight ovoid shape. Wickerwork design, in relief casting, and chased. Various insects modeled in relief. Side handles of bamboo pattern.

Signed on the foot.

Height, 13 inches.

No. 131
BRONZE GROUP

40—

"Horse and Cat," by Frémiet. Rich brown patina.

Signed.

Height, 6 inches; length, 8 inches.

No. 132

BRONZE FIGURE

"The Little Fisherman," by Gemito, a Neapolitan sculptor, who, when young, visited Paris at Meissonier's invitation. The great painter thought so highly of him that he entertained him at his house and kept him as a guest as long as he could.

Signed proof, *cire perdue*.

Height, 10 inches; diameter, 10 inches.

No. 133

BRONZE STATUETTE

"Croquet," by d'Épinay. Brown patina.

Signed.

Height, 10½ inches.

No. 134

PAIR BRONZE STATUETTES

"The Gladiators," by Gérôme. Antique green patina.

Signed.

Height, 17 inches.

No. 135

JAPANESE BRONZE COVERED VASE

Wickerwork design, cast and chiseled. Skillfully wrought, lifelike rats and mice in bold relief. Fine patina.

Height, 11 inches; diameter, 12 inches.

No. 136

BRONZE STATUETTE

"Meissonier," by d'Épinay. Brown patina with green markings.

Signed.   Height, 11 inches.

No. 137

BRONZE STATUETTE

"Woman of the First Empire," by Gemito. Green patina.

Signed proof, *cire perdue*.   Height, 21 inches.

No. 138

BRONZE EQUESTRIAN FIGURE

"Duc d'Orleans," by Frémiet. Brown patina.

Signed.   Height, 19 inches; width, 15 inches.

No. 139

BRONZE BUST

"The Fisher Boy," by Gemito. With bronze and gilt pedestal.

Signed proof, *cire perdue*.   Height, 20 inches; diameter, 11 inches.

No. 140

BRONZE EQUESTRIAN FIGURE

"Gaston de Foix," by Barye. Fine green patina.

Signed proof from Barye's studio.

Height, 14 inches; length, 13 inches.

405 —

No. 141

BRONZE ORNAMENTAL PEDESTAL

By Barye. Byzantine design, oval-shape, green patina, black marble top.

From Barye's studio.

Height, 7 inches; length, 18 inches.

105

No. 142

BRONZE GROUP

"St. George and the Dragon," by Frémiet. Gilt finish, with white marble base.

Signed.

Height, 22 inches; width, 15 inches.

210

No. 143

BRONZE GROUP

"Panther Seizing a Stag," by Barye. Fine green patina.

Signed proof from Barye's studio.

Height, 15 inches; length, 22 inches.

1,200

No. 144

BRONZE GROUP

"Tiger Seizing a Deer," by Barye. Fine green patina.

Signed proof from Barye's studio.

Height, 13 inches; length, 23 inches.

1,375 -

No. 145

TERRA COTTA BUST

"Paul Baudry," by Dubais.

Signed.

Life size.

No. 146

TERRA COTTA BUST

"Jean Léon Gérôme," by Carpeaux.

Signed. Dated 1873.

Life size.

No. 147

MANTEL CLOCK

Green marble case, surmounted by group of "Fawn and Cub Bears," sculptured in white marble by Frémiet.

Height, 20 inches; length, 24 inches.

Signed.

No. 148

PAIR BRONZE CANDELABRAS

By Cain. Bamboo tripod design, with snail feet; mice and bird-nest ornamentation in relief.

Signed.

Height, 20 inches.

No. 149

PAIR ELABORATE BRONZE VASES

Japanese. Tall ovoid shape, with bold, flaring necks; cast and chiseled relief ornamentation of dragons, birds, and clouds; gold inlays, elephant-head handles.

Height, including stands, 37 inches; diameter, 15 inches.

No. 150

346 — each

PAIR LARGE CLOISONNÉ VASES

Old Chinese. Grand bottle-shape. Designs of lotus plants in bloom, and birds in green, turquoise, and white enamel on a ground of Indian red. Fitted as lamps.

Height, 23 inches; diameter, 17 inches.

No. 151

375

LOUIS XVI. CABINET

Inlaid with various woods; elaborately wrought brass mountings; door ornamented with finely decorated Sèvres porcelain medallions; white marble top.

Height, 45 inches; length, 55 inches.

No. 152

LARGE TABLE

400 —

Inlaid with ivory and various woods; elaborately carved supports.

Height, 32 inches; length, 60 inches; width, 48 inches.

No. 153

TWO ELABORATE ARMCHAIRS

To match the above-described table.

No. 154

FOUR HIGH-BACK CHAIRS

To match the foregoing.

No. 155

EIGHTEENTH CENTURY DUTCH SCREEN

700

Carved and beautifully lacquered by Japanese artists. Four folds.

Height, 75 inches; length, 108 inches.

THE AMERICAN ART ASSOCIATION,

Managers

THOMAS E. KIRBY,

Auctioneer

List of Artists Represented and Their Works

ARTIST	SUBJECT	CATALOGUE NUMBER
ALMA-TADEMA, L.	Roman Youth Reading Horace	13
ARCOS, S.	Buffoon	32
BAUDRY, P. J. A.	Parisina	49
	The Wave and the Pearl	69
	Fortune and the Child	103
BELLANGÉ, J. L. H.	Military Sketches	1
BENLLIURE, J.	House at Naples	81
BOLDINI, G.	River Seine at Mont-Valérian	15
	The Rest at the Studio	21
	Clichy Square, Paris	58
	The Beach at Etrétat	82
	Pond in the Forest of Fontainebleau	90
	River Seine at Bougival	104
	Highway of Combes-la-Ville	115
BONNAT, L. J. F.	Neapolitan Peasants at the Farnese Palace	63
BONINGTON, R. P.	View of Old Paris	19
BONVIN, L.	Wild Flowers	18
CHAM	The Commune	7
CLAYS, P. J.	On the Coast	8
	Dead Calm	105

ARTIST	SUBJECT	CATALOGUE NUMBER
COOSEMANS, J. T.	Summer Landscape	50
	Winter Landscape	59
COROT, J. B. C.	Ville d'Avray	33
	Sunset	98
DAUBIGNY, C. F.	Auvers on the Oise	35
DECAMPS, A. G.	Death and the Woodman	97
DUEZ, E. A.	The Pont Neuf, Paris	67
DUPRAY, H. L.	Waterloo	66
FIRMAN-GIRARD	Parisian Flower-Girl	53
FORTUNY, M.	Corpus Christi	5
	Study of Flowers	10
	The Arquebusier	16
	Arab Fantasia	27
	Italian Peasant Girl	31
	Arab's Head	40
	Café of the Swallows	44
	One of the "King's Moors"	52
	The Old Peasant	56
	Court of Justice, Alhambra	61
	Courtyard, Alhambra	68
	Arab at Prayer	74
	Gipsy Caves, Granada	80
	Breakfast in the Old Convent Yard	85
	Rosa Contadina	91
	Arab Reclining on a Divan	94
	The Masquerade	102
	A Street in Tangiers	106
	Meissonier's Portrait	111
	The Choice of a Model	114
	Dead Girl	116
	The Antiquary	119
	Arab Butcher	121

ARTIST	SUBJECT	CATALOGUE NUMBER
FORTUNY, M.	Environs de Tanger	124
	The Alberca Court, Alhambra	127
GAVARNI	Small Talk	78
GÉRÔME, J. L.	Door of a Mosque, with Heads of Decapitated Rebels	39
GREGORY, E. J.	The War in the East	2
HARPIGNIES, H.	Autumn. Castle of San Angelo	6
HEILBUTH, F.	Monte Pincio	11
	Lady in Yellow	62
	San Giovanni Laterano	79
HERNANDEZ, DON G.	Head of a Girl	45
HORSCHELT, T.	An Arabian Horseman	42
KNAUS, L.	The Landlord	71
LAMI, L. E.	Off for the Hunt	77
LEIBL, W.	Village Politicians	118
MACCARI, C.	Women at Raphael's Tomb	29
MADRAZO, R. DE	Woman and Parrot	26
	Woman and Guitar	37
	Departure from the Masked Ball	120
	Pierrette	128
MEISSONIER, J. L. E.	Italian Armor, Sixteenth Century	75
	Armor	76
	The End of a Game of Cards	110
	The Stirrup Cup	112
MENZEL, A. F. E.	The Stirrup Cup	9
MICHETTI, F. P.	A Seaside Idyl	48
	The Turkey Girl	60
	Spring	96
MOORE, H. HUMPHREY	Banks of a River	17

ARTIST	SUBJECT	CATALOGUE NUMBER
MORELLI, D.	Woman Seated	73
MESZÖLY, G. VON	Farm Scene	23
NITTIS, G. de	Lowlands Near Naples	36
	Route from Brindisi to Barletta	107
PARSONS, A.	English Landscape	25
PETTENKOFEN, A. VON	A Market in Hungary	83
	Hungarian Peasant Wagon	89
PILLE, H.	Lansquenets	3
PINWELL, G. J.	Rural Life, England	54
RIBERA, R.	Café Chantant	14
	Café Ambulant	95
RICO, M.	Venetian Canal with View of Veronese's Tomb	12
	Fisherman, Seville	20
	Boats at Poissy	30
	A Spanish Garden	43
	Pond at Meaux	57
	The Tarpeian Rock, Rome	84
	The Woodcutter	87
	Seville	92
	Plaza and Street, Toledo	108
	Avenue Josephine Market, Paris	109
	Rienzi's House in Rome	113
ROMAKO, A.	The Huntress	126
ROTHSCHILD, BARONESS C. de	View of Capri	55
ROUSSEAU, T.	The Woodcutter, Forest of Fontainebleau	99
ROYBET, F. V. L.	The Kitchen in the Castle	65
SANT, J.	Gipsy Fortune Teller	70

ARTIST	SUBJECT	CATALOGUE NUMBER
SMALL, W.	A Plowing Match	4
STEVENS, A.	Alsace	28
	Woman and Elephant	51
	Remembrance and Regrets	93
STEWART, J. L.	Summer	123
TROYON, C.	Valley of the Toucques	34
	Chickens Feeding	46
	The Lane	100
	Cow Among the Cabbages	117
VAN LERIUS, J. H. F.	An Old Woman's Head	38
VAN MARCKE, É.	A Normandy Cow	47
	Cows in the Valley, Toucques	122
VIERGE, D.	The Bridle Path, Bois de Boulogne	72
VOLLON, A.	Crystal Bowl and Fruit	64
	Monkey and Fruit	125
WEBER, O.	Plowing	22
	Landscape and Cows	88
ZAMACOÏS, E.	Fortuny's Model	24
	The Infanta	41
	The Snowball	86
	Checkmated	101

www.ingramcontent.com/pod-product-compliance
Lightning Source LLC
Chambersburg PA
CBHW020249170426
43202CB00008B/295